THE CONTEMPORARY DISCUSSION SERIES

GOD AND TEMPORALITY

GOD

THE CONTEMPORARY DISCUSSION SERIES

GOD AND TEMPORALITY

Edited by Bowman L. Clarke & Eugene T. Long

NEW ERA BOOKS
Paragon House Publishers
New York

Paragon House Publishers, Inc.
866 Second Avenue
New York, New York 10017
First edition © 1984. All rights reserved
Printed in the United States of America

ISBN 0-913757-10-1 Pbk.
ISBN 0-913757-11-X

To Our Scotts

Scott Booth and Scott Long

CONTENTS

Preface   ix

Introduction   1
  Bowman L. Clarke

PART ONE

God As Love   15
  Brian P. Gaybba

The Divine Historicity   37
  Galen A. Johnson

Does Divine Love Entail Suffering In God?   55
  William J. Hill

Over-Power and God's Responsibility for Sin   73
  Nelson C. Pike

The Feminine Images of God in Shusaku Endo   99
  Jean Higgins

PART TWO

God and Temporality: A Heideggerian View   121
  Eugene T. Long

Time and Eternity in Royce and Bergson   133
  Milič Čapek

God as Alpha and Omega: Dipolar Theism   155
  Gene Reeves

God as Process in Whitehead   169
  Bowman L. Clarke

Contributors   189

PREFACE

Since the middle of the nineteenth century Western philosophers and theologians have become accustomed to talking of the transcendence and immanence of God. The term 'transcendence' is used to point to the otherness of God to the world, to God's absolute priority to created entities. This way of talking about God is aligned with many of the attributes assigned to God in classical theism where God is understood, for example, to be timeless, immutable, and impassible. In some sense, however, God has also been held to be immanent, to be active in creation, to be concerned with the creatures of the world. Much of the emphasis in discussions of the concept of God during the first half of the twentieth century focused on the otherness of God and the infinite qualitative difference between God and the world. This approach often tended to lead in the direction of an asymmetrical relation between God and the world. In recent discussions, a more organic understanding of the relation between God and his creatures seems to be at the forefront of discussions concerning the concept of God. This latter is the concern of this group of essays.

All but one of these essays, the essay of Milič Čapek, were read at a meeting on "God: The Contemporary Discussion," held at Fort Lauderdale, Florida, in 1983 and sponsored by the New Ecumenical Research Association. The editors wish to thank the authors of the essays for permission to include their work and thank New ERA for its help in collecting and publishing the essays. The editors also wish to thank *Revue Internationale de Philosophie* for permission to reprint Čapek's essay.

Eugene T. Long
and Bowman L. Clarke

Introduction

Bowman L. Clarke

The title *God and Temporality* was chosen for this group of essays, rather than the title *God and Time,* because the term 'temporality' has a more concrete connotation than the term 'time'. Time can be thought of in a very abstract sense, for example, merely as an ordering of events, or instants, in terms of some relation such as earlier than or before. The term 'temporality', on the other hand, has a far richer connotation and suggests all the concrete conditions of temporal existence, i.e., time as experienced in the concrete. It is God's relation to the latter which is the theme that runs through this collection of essays and ties them together. Despite the differences in religious background, philosophic orientation, and vocabulary of the authors considered in the second section, together they represent a call to take more seriously God's involvement in temporality, particularly human temporal existence, and to work out the problems which arise from so doing.

In the first essay, "God As Love," Brian Gaybba argues that if we take seriously God's love, it can revolutionize our thinking about the Divinity. He does this by proposing that love is the essence of God. He does not maintain that to do so will provide any final solutions to the age-old theological problems of human freedom and the divine concursus, the problem of evil, etc.; the point of his argument is that God's relation to the temporal creatures, along

1

with age-old problems this gives rise to, will be taken more seriously. The inevitable result, he thinks, will be an altering of our thinking about what God is like, as well as our experience of God's activity in the temporal world.

As far as thinking about what God is like, Gaybba first argues that God must be taken as social, or interpersonal. Although it may appear at first that Gaybba is speaking of God as a network of relations, it becomes clear that he is speaking of a community related by love. Secondly, this will lead us to rethink our notion of divine simplicity. Thirdly, he argues that we will have to rethink our idea of divine omnipotence. For in taking the essence of God to be love, the only power God has is love—and love is essentially kenotic. God will limit the divine power for the freedom of the creatures God loves. Thus human freedom and the openness of the future will be taken more seriously. Fourthly, we will think of God as respecting the temporality of the temporal creatures, and this will in turn affect our view of divine omnipotence. God, as related to me this moment, cannot from that relationship know with infallible certainty what I will do tomorrow. Fifthly, we will be led to rethink our view of God's impassibility. God must be affected by the needs and suffering of the temporal creatures. God will suffer. Sixthly, all this implies a radical change from traditional conceptions of the divine immutability. Rather than interpreting it in terms of changelessness, we will be led to interpret it in terms of the constancy of divine love. Seventhly, we will be led to see the divine unity in that which is created in and through the loving relationships. As far as our experience of God in the temporal world, Gaybba maintains that if love is to be taken to be the essence of God, then love will be taken to be the sign of God's presence, and it will also become the test for evaluating different claims of revelations of God.

In "The Divine Historicity," Galen Johnson takes the Gaybba theme further. By focusing on the concept of person and its applicability to God, he argues that we must be willing to speak of the historicity of God, and he maintains that this is even more the case in any incarnational religion such as Christianity. In speaking of historical, or temporal, existence, Johnson means an existence in which past acts are cumulatively retained and future acts anticipated "in presence," such that the description of the meaning of a present action presupposes a description of the relevant past and future. We act with reference to some past and in anticipation of some future. In short, "presence," in contrast to "a present," has thickness, or duration, and it involves a relevant past sedimented in it and a future anticipation in it. The historical existence of a person, for Johnson, is far richer than even this. Persons are self-constituting, or self-making beings; that is, they are free. They make a world which they transcend, as well as a world of relations to other persons which they surpass. This world and the world of relations to other persons is made within the limits of a natural and historical situation. Whatever one may think of Johnson's analysis of person-hood and of historical existence, one would have to agree that it is most difficult, if not impossible, to conceive of a person who does not freely act on the basis of an accumulated past and anticipating a future, who does not exist in an environment of persons and nonpersons to which he is related, and who is not limited to a natural and historical situation.

Johnson then raises the question of the compatibility of historical existence, so analyzed, with the divine reality, and finds that the idea of God as historical ought to be taken more seriously than it has been. He accepts the fact, however, that there must be some important qualifications concerning the historicity of God. God is not limited to a natural and historical situation as are finite persons, since God is eternal. Likewise, there is no past prior to God or future after God as with finite persons. God's limitations must be self-limitations, they are not limitations in which God is thrown as with finite persons. Thus for Johnson, God is not historical *per se,* but God is superhistorical. God is historical without the imper-fections, or limitations, of finite historicity, which he interprets as a dialectical synthesis of the affirmation "God is historical" and its negation, "God is not historical."

Gaybba's discussion of God's essence as love and Johnson's analysis of the concept of person as applied to God are strong arguments that God's involvement in temporality must be taken seriously and that this has serious consequences for how we conceive of God. This point is, however, well balanced by William Hill's essay, "Does Divine Love Entail Suffering in God?". Hill wishes also to take God's involvement in temporality seriously, but he cautions us not to give up those attributes usually associated with

3

the transcendence of God, such as impassibility and immutability. On the contrary, he maintains that it is precisely God's utter transcendence of and autonomy from the world that explains his universal and intimate involvement with every finite reality and event in the temporal world. He mentions a number of attempts in contemporary theology and philosophy to take God's involvement in temporality seriously, but he focuses primarily on Jürgen Moltmann and the theme of suffering in God. In so doing, he presents a strong case that we must hold on to both God's transcendence and the attributes traditionally associated with it, as well as God's loving relationship to the finite temporal creatures. He proposes holding these two in tension by maintaining that God does not suffer in his divinity, but that God does suffer in and through the humanity God has made one with himself. In this way he hopes to be able to say that the suffering which God truly experiences does not result in any qualitative change or diminution of the divine nature, and consequently to hold on to the divine immutability and impassibility without denying the claim that God wills to suffer in and through the suffering of his temporal creatures. In this way God is not subject to change, as are the temporal creatures; God remains unchangeably God. It is the very transcendence of God, Hill maintains, that makes it possible for God to fully experience the suffering of the temporal creature in and through the humanity he has made one with himself; that is, God can love unfathomably because it is no threat to God's own divine being. This Hill takes to be a genuine Christian panentheism, in which God who lies beyond suffering in his divinity nevertheless loves and chooses freely to suffer as man for mankind.

Nelson Pike, in his essay "Over-Power and God's Responsibility for Sin," focuses on one of the age-old problems of theology which inevitably arises when we take seriously God's relation to the temporal creation, a creation seriously flawed by evil. Pike considers only moral evil, or sin, and argues that that which is usually called the free-will defense cannot absolve God of responsibility for sin. Pike proposes to explicate the concept of omnipotence in terms of what he calls "over-power"—the power to determine which, if any, powers are possessed by agents other than oneself. If God is omnipotent, or has over-power, yet creates free creatures that sin, although he may not be said to be the cause of their sin, God can be said to be responsible in a real sense for their sin. In short, the free-will defense does not free God of the responsibility for moral evil. The way in which Pike presents his argument here rests upon his contention that God could have created agents who do not have the power to sin and yet are free agents; that is, are still free to choose between alternatives. They would be free agents, though not free only with respect to the performance of a specific range of actions, namely, wrong actions. An adequate theodicy, Pike argues, cannot avoid God's responsibility for sin and must move to a higher level to answer the question: Should God be blamed for sin? God can only be absolved of blame in terms of some higher good which justifies the creator's allowing the free creatures to perform immoral acts.

One may wish to question Pike's argument that God can create free creatures who are still not free to sin, since such freedom would be morally vacuous. The creature would be free only to choose between alternatives which are of equal moral value. Suppose we characterize a morally free agent, which seems to be the real concern of the free-will defense, as one who has the power to choose between alternatives of unequal moral value; and then argue that God could not create free moral agents that do not have the power to sin. This would weaken, or perhaps destroy, the force of Pike's particular argument; nevertheless, there is still a problem. We still have not absolved God from all blame so long as God creates freely. We have merely removed the problem to a different level. We must also argue that there is greater potentiality for value resulting from the creation of morally free agents than from the creation of Pike's free agents. In short, the whole problem of evil boils down to this: Do the potentialities for value in creation outweigh the risks for evil? If we argue that this is the case, however, we are faced with another question: Is a God who is indifferent to the suffering that results from these risks for evil in creation a God who is worthy of worship? Unless God shares in that suffering, have we presented little more than an empty intellectual solution to the problem of evil in God's temporal creation? It is at this point of the problem of evil that the question of God's involvement in temporality is most keenly felt.

Although the problem of evil is an age-old problem in theodicy, the contemporary feminists are raising the new problem of male and female images in our talk about God. In "The Feminine Image of God in Shasaku Endo," Jean Higgins explores the use of female imagery for God in one writer. There are a number of things that Higgins's essay contributes to the theme of taking God's relation to temporality seriously. First, it stresses the fact that those characteristics, apart from the strictly biological ones which are not applicable to God, which we associate with the female and male images are largely historically and culturally conditioned. Second, those images which we choose to apply to God, either male or female, not only characterize God for us, they in turn influence and condition history. Consider, for example, the almost universal use of the pronoun 'he' in referring to God. Those characteristics which we, by cultural and historical conditioning, associate with the male are brought to the fore in the way in which we think of God. And in turn, this reinforces those characteristics and the male role in our culture and history. Third, the female images which are usually applied to God emphasize those characteristics of God which portray his involvement in temporality, i.e., creating, self-sacrificial loving, forgiving, gentle, passive, peace making, patient, long suffering, etc. Higgins's essay is a call for those who wish to take God's involvement with temporality seriously to take a serious look at the use of female images for God, as well as to look at what we have done in the past by not taking female images for God seriously. Endo is only one such example.

In *Process and Reality* Whitehead wrote: "Religion should connect the rational generality of philosophy with the emotions and purposes springing out of existence in a particular society, in a particular epoch, and conditioned by particular antecedents."[1] The previous group of essays are religious in that sense. They grow out of religious problems, or themes, that have arisen in a particular society, in a particular epoch, and are conditioned by particular antecedents, but they seek the rational generality of philosophy to articulate them and to justify them. The second group of essays are more philosophical in nature, for they concern several men who have proposed general schemes of ideas which have a certain generality of applicability in human experience. The essays explore how the question of involvement of God in temporality might appear in their philosophical schemes. One could pose the question of these essays in this way: How is God's eternity related

6

to temporality?

In the first essay in this group, "God and Temporality: A Heideggerian View," Eugene Long reflects many of the concerns of Johnson. He too focuses upon the concept of a person and uses Heidegger's concept of Dasein, or temporality, to explicate the concept of a person. He then follows a suggestion of Heidegger that God's eternity should be a primordial infinite temporality. Long begins by pointing to Heidegger's distinction between clock time, which is little more than an ordering of instants in terms of the relation, earlier than, or what was referred to earlier as the most abstract notion of time, and temporality. Persons are involved in time at a level quite different from clock time; it is time as we experience it in the concrete, or temporality. In order to explicate temporality, Long uses Heidegger's threefold structure of possibility, facticity, and falling to explicate Dasein and how its possibilities are grounded in temporality. Dasein is in some sense ahead of itself, projecting its possibilities (possibility); it is not *de novo*, it is already there, thrown into a world (facticity); and it is absorbed in its present (falling). This is not merely an abstract future, past, and present; it is the way persons in the world concretely experience their past, future, and present.

Long, in applying this structure of temporality to God cautions us, however, that it is not the finite temporality of human persons that we wish to apply to God, but a primordial infinite temporality. This would make God, he suggests, more than temporal; God's temporality in some sense must transcend and include within itself the temporality of finite persons. God is not bounded, or limited, by time; God is not *in* time. This raises, however, an interesting question. One of the characteristics of the structure of finite temporality is possibility, how one will be in a future which is not yet settled. It may be, as Long suggests, that God unifies within himself all the finite anticipated futures and remembered pasts, and in this sense temporality is included in God. But does God merely include all finite anticipated futures, with no future of his own, or does God have anticipated futures of his own? The question may be put this way: Is there only one present for God with no futurity of its own, but embracing the many finite "presents"; or are there a number of "presents" for God, each with its own futurity? Long appears to opt for the latter when he quotes from

Macquarrie, suggesting that at every point new vistas will open up for God. This seems to suggest that God constantly faces a new, open future of his own.

In his essay, "Time and Eternity in Royce and Bergson," Milič Čapek finds in these two men two alternative ways in which futurity can be related to God's eternity. Čapek first focuses on the similarities between Royce and Bergson. Both men view time primarily as it is concretely experienced, rather than the mere abstract ordering of instants in terms of earlier than, or later than; they both see the latter as a conceptual construction from the former. Both men would agree that the so-called "specious present," which is the concrete datum we experience, is the "real present" and the "instant present" which we construct, the "specious present." Both men also agree that by increasing the concretely experienced present we move in the direction in which eternity, a concentration of all duration, lies. Thus both men differ from the traditional notion that eternity is instantaneous, involving no duration, or no earlier and later than ordering.

Despite their agreement, however, Čapek sees a very important difference between the way in which Royce and Bergson view eternity, or this limitless duration. For Royce there is only one "now," or specious present; for his Absolute there is no future beyond that present, no awareness of something yet to come for the Absolute. It is an all-inclusive present, even though it includes all finite specious presents and their futurity. There is only futurity, a yet to be, relative to the finite components within it. Thus the specious present for Royce's Absolute differs radically from our own. Because of this Čapek questions whether or not this abolishes time's direction, since the future loses its character of genuine futurity. The open and "not yet" character of the immediate future enters into the constitution of any event. Čapek also takes a consequence of this to be that it leaves no place for becoming, or divine self-creation. In contrast, Čapek sees Bergson as having a "moving" character to his eternity. It is a "living" and "growing" eternity. He sees this eternity as made up of smaller durations each including the past, but its forward edge is always "bounded" by an unrealized future. Here, however, Čapek raises a serious question as to whether or not to speak of such as eternity is no more than a mere *façon de paler*, for it always has a "not yet." How is it an infinite, or unlimited, duration if it is always bounded toward the future?

In the last two papers this contrast which Čapek sees between Royce and Bergson is developed further in a contrast between Whitehead and Hartshorne. In "God as Alpha and Omega: Dipolar Process Theism," Gene Reeves presents Hartshorne's view of God. He begins in true Hartshornean fashion by presenting a list of general polar metaphysical terms, such as, 'abstract' and 'concrete', 'absolute' and 'relative', 'being' and 'becoming', 'eternal' and 'temporal'. He christens the first term in each pair of the list an alpha term and the other an omega term. He then points to two traditional assumptions about these alpha and omega terms. First, it has traditionally been assumed that one cannot truly predicate both an alpha and an omega term of the same individual. Second, it has been assumed that anything of which an alpha term is truly predicated is both ontologically and axiologically superior to anything of which the contrasting omega term is truly predicated. Hartshorne has seriously questioned both of these assumptions in theology and philosophy. So Reeves considers Hartshorne's dipolar theism to be a reversal of these two traditional assumptions, so that both sets of terms are applicable to God in different respects. God is, for example, both abstract and concrete, both absolute and relative, God both is and is becoming, both is eternal and is temporal, but in all cases in different respects. Reeves then argues for the superiority of this dipolar concept of God in terms of rational coherence, consistency with our ordinary experience, and in terms of value theory and religious experience. It is here that he approaches most clearly the concerns of the essays of the first part.

Only in passing, however, does Reeves mention the distinction between the two contrasting ways of conceiving of God's temporality which was the concern of Čapek's paper. Reeves speaks of the difference between Whitehead and Hartshorne in terms of whether or not God is to be thought of as a single actual entity (Whitehead) or as a personally ordered series of actual occasions, a living divine person (Hartshorne). The contrast here is analogous to Čapek's contrast between Royce and Bergson. It is the presentation of Whitehead's view that is the concern of Bowman Clarke's paper, "God as Process in Whitehead." Clarke begins by distinguishing the two types of process in Whitehead, the process of transition and the genetic process. The process of transition is the process of temporal

9

transpiring. The genetic process is the process of becoming, or the actualization of an actual entity. The former process is temporal with earlier and later portions; the latter is nontemporal in that its stages are not ordered in terms of earlier and later than. In order to explicate these two types of process, Clarke takes advantage of MacTaggert's series A and series B in his paradox of time. Whitehead's own position may be summarized this way: The actualization of an event, or a segment of time, and its perishing is not itself an event, and consequently has no temporal transpiring. This distinction between the transpiring of an event, which of course is temporal, and the becoming or actualization of an event, which is nontemporal, gives Whitehead an answer to Čapek's question with reference to Royce: If there is only one present for God with no past or future of its own, even though it includes all finite presents with their own pasts and futures, how can God become or be self-creative? Whitehead's answer is that the transpiring of the duration which is God's present is distinguishable from its becoming. Thus God *per se* does not, strictly speaking, change. God merely becomes what God is, and in becoming includes all temporal duration; and even though this temporal transpiring which is God's duration includes all change, it itself does not change. Clarke suggests that what is needed here to treat the problem clearly is a tense logic, based not on instants, but events with duration and limited to a place in space—that is "here-nows" with temporal and spatial thickness to them—and a tense logic based on the space-time of relativity theory rather than an absolute time.

Clarke ends his essay with a schema of levels of divine involvement in temporality, a schema which orders the various philosophical positions presented in the second group of essays. There is the traditional position in which eternity is seen as including all time in one simultaneous whole with no earlier and later ordering. This is the position of least temporal involvement by the deity (St. Thomas). Then there is the position in which God includes all temporal duration in one present, in which earlier and later than is preserved for the finite presents which it includes, but that infinite present has no past or future of its own, since it includes all temporal duration (Royce and Whitehead). Then there is also the position in which God includes all time, but has a sequence of divine presents each with its own open future. This is the level of the greatest divine involvement in temporality (Bergson and Hartshorne).

When we take all these essays as a group, we can see that the philosophical essays of the second group are offering schema for God's involvement in temporality that can be useful in articulating the problems raised by the first group of essays. It is not the purpose of this introduction to evaluate these alternative schema in the light of this purpose; this will be a task left for the reader. Much, however, will depend upon how well Čapek's questions can be answered. Does, for example, the Royce-Whitehead schema abolish the direction of time and, in Bergson's phrase, spatialize it? Does it allow God's becoming and temporal transition to make sense? Does the Bergson-Hartshorne schema make God's eternity an eternity in name only and, in fact, reduce God to a finite temporal creature? These questions need further serious reflection. What cannot be ignored, however, is the call which all of these essays make to take God's involvement in temporality seriously and to work out the problems which this presents.

NOTES

1 Alfred North Whitehead, *Process and Reality* (New York: Macmillan, 1941), 23.

PART ONE

God As Love

Brian P. Gaybba

T he theme "God is love," curiously neglected throughout
Christian history, has received increasing attention in recent
years.[1] However, the attention devoted to it is still mini-
mal in comparison to what one would have thought its importance
for Christian thought. For what follows I cannot claim very much
originality. My purpose is simply to disseminate still further
interest in the topic by: (a) arguing that love is God's essence, not an
attribute or activity thereof, and (b) drawing out some of the implications this has for our understanding of what God is like and our
experience of divine activity in the world.

Love as God's Essence

Of course, for traditional Christian natural theology, the
distinction between the divine essence and its attributes has always
been regarded as artificial. The affirmation of God's absolute
simplicity entailed the affirmation that the distinction between the
divine essence and attributes was made by us because of the way in
which we know and experience God, but that in fact God's essence
and his attributes were one and the same. If one accepts that, then
the issue becomes rather this: what is more *appropriately* described
as essence, and what as attributes?

As regards the distinction between the two, we could do worse

15

than quote the old scholastics. According to them, essence was *id quo res est id quod est*—that by which a thing was what it was. Attributes, on the other hand, are those things that flow necessarily from this essence. The essence is logically prior to the attributes. When we talk about God's essence, therefore, we are talking about what *from our point of view* makes God God. Or, to put it another way, we are searching for "the primary and foremost characteristic by which man recognizes God as God."[2]

What is that characteristic? The chief Christian practitioners of this debate, the scholastics (old and new), differed in their opinions. There were those who said it was God's infinity, others that it was the divine intelligence, while others opted for absolute liberty. The most favored viewpoint, especially in recent scholasticism, was that God's essence was to be found in the divine *aseity* (i.e., in the fact that the divine exists in and of itself), or, which really boiled down to the same thing, God's *self-subsistence*. God was defined as self-subsistent Being. Few authors, it seems, opted for the idea that God's essence was love.[3] And yet, there it stands in black and white in the Christian scriptures: "God is love."

It is frequently pointed out that the author of the letter did not intend this as an abstract definition of the divine essence. No doubt the reason for the warning is to prevent us from imposing philosophical abstractions onto the biblical text. Neither God nor his essence are ever abstractions for the biblical tradition. However, it would be equally wrong to see in 1 John's phrase simply a strong way of saying that God loves us. The grammatical form "God is love" seems to be deliberately intended to describe God's basic nature—his essence—though in a vibrant way, one that brings out clearly God's personal character. C. H. Dodd[4] pointed out that the author of the epistle may very likely have been familiar with attempts that had been made to define the divinity in terms of its characteristic activity, for essences are revealed by their activities. First John's statement could well have been his way of doing what others had done. And since for Christians God's characteristic activity was love, God's essence was said to be that.

For Christians it therefore makes good *theological* sense to describe God's essence as love. And to do so is to say that all the divine attributes (from our point of view) are aspects of that love—which is the exact opposite of the idea that his love is (from our point of view) only an attribute of a more fundamental reality, such as "self-subsistent Being." However, I think it also makes good *metaphysical* sense. I will have to simply beg the question whether metaphysics makes any sense at all. I believe it not only makes sense but is essential to all sense. But I also believe cosmological ideas have influenced metaphysicians more than many of them (certainly the past ones) would have cared to admit.

The route to being has always been being as it has been experienced by us. And the way we experience being will be colored by our cosmology. Scholastic metaphysics inherited an Aristotelian cosmology, one that saw reality as composed of discrete, clearly divisible entities—a world of objects. They may or may not depend on each other. But all were striking in their limitations. They all had one or other kind of limit. Ultimate Being was also viewed more or less as an object, but one whose distinctiveness was to be found in its lack of limitations. Its essence could therefore be seen as residing in its total independence and self-sufficiency. Today's cosmology is different. Physics has revealed reality to us as a network of dynamic interrelationships. Moreover, what is so interrelated is ultimately not a solid thing but energy. Reality is a constant interchange of energy patterns, some, from our perspective, more stable than others. Matching this cosmology is today's widespread emphasis on the essential interrelatedness of humanity, manifested especially in interpersonal relationships, the heart of which is love. Our experience of reality on all levels, therefore, is an experience of interrelatedness. Moreover, our experience of personal reality is such that we (in the West at any rate—I do not wish to exclude the East: I just do not know) would find it difficult to conceive of it enjoying fulfillment without love. In short, interrelatedness, which on a personal level finds conscious expression in love, seems to us from an experiential point of view to be the structure of being. Such interrelatedness is not necessarily seen as a sign of finitude (as the medievals would have and did see multiplicity), but as something that could characterize the Absolute itself. It makes more sense for us therefore to conceive of the absolute in such terms.

Anyway, I am not a philosopher and so must leave to others the task of building a metaphysics on the basis of contemporary physics. My main point in this section has been to show that a description of God's essence as love makes good theological and metaphysical sense. What for us makes God God is not the bald fact of being uncaused, but that, unlike anything else, God does not merely show love but is love. As such God is the source or ground of that which we value—in our better moments anyway—more than anything else.

Let us see what this implies for our understanding of what God is like.

Implications for Our Understanding of What God Is Like

The first implication concerns *the meaning of the word "God."* If one holds that God does need creatures in order to be God, then it seems to me that the inevitable implication of regarding God's essence as love is that the word "God" cannot refer to a single personal identity. Whatever views one may have regarding the love that humans experience as more valuable than all other things, it is that it exists between persons. One has then to admit of some sort of inter*personal* relationship within God. One is drawn inevitably to the idea that the word "God" refers not to a person but to a network of interpersonal relationships. This implies more than one "person" "in" God.

This introduces an ambiguity into the use of the word "God," one that can generate considerable confusion. This confusion is already a feature of Christian usage of the word. Ever since Christians abandoned the New Testament practice of reserving the word "God" for the Father (although even in the New Testament there are exceptions to this), a confusion entered into their language that has bred a parallel confusion in thought. Who, for example, is being referred to when Christian writers refer to God as "he": the divine nature, the Father, the Son, the Spirit (who form the Christian trinity), all three? Or take the well-known Christian assertion: "God became man." Here the word "God" does not mean quite what it means in the New Testament, for it does not refer to the one Jesus called "Father" and his forefathers "Yahweh" but rather to Jesus himself who, Christians believe, is the incarnation of one of three "persons" in God, each of whom is equally entitled to the appellation "God."

How to resolve this linguistic confusion in a satisfactory way is difficult to say. To revert to the New Testament practice of reserving the word to "the Father" will be seen as derogating from the divinity of the other two members of the trinity. To speak of "they" sounds grammatically odd if the plural pronoun is in a sentence where its referent is the singular "God." To speak of "the divinity" or the "Godhead" when one wishes to refer to the interpersonal network itself has the merit of greater clarity. The trouble arises, however, when one wishes to speak of divine actions, for *actiones sunt suppositorum*—actions attributed to agents, not simply to natures. Hence one can hardly avoid using personal pronouns.

The purpose of this paper is not to suggest a solution. The main point of the present section is not the ambiguity but the fact that if God *is* love, then the divinity is structured interpersonally. However, I must for the rest of the paper adopt some practical solution to the ambiguity created thereby. Hence, for the sake of convenience, whenever I wish to talk of a divine activity or attitude I will retain the practice of using singular verbs. Moreover, for the sake of clarity I will regard such verbs as having as their referent the one whom the Christian tradition holds to be the source of all things, including the relational life within the divinity: i.e., the one whom the Jews of old called "Yahweh," Jesus called "Father," and the Muslims call "Allah." However, it is worth stressing that if God is love (and here one can, if one wishes, rephrase it to say "if the Father is love"), then the Father's being can only be understood in relational terms—i.e., in relation to the person or persons to whom he relates in love. Incidentally, to say that the *Father* is love does not necessarily imply that he himself is a network of interpersonal relationships. Love indeed demands relationships. Hence to say "x is love" means that x cannot be x without a relationship. But if "God" (including in the term not only a subject of attribution but also the stuff that is divinity) is love, then one must hold *either* that God needs creatures to be fully God (which some indeed hold to be the case) *or* (if one cannot accept that assertion, as I do not) that divinity is itself structured interpersonally. To say then that God is love is to say that what we call "God" is in fact a community. This, incidentally, gives added depth to the statement that man was made "in God's image" (Gen. 1:26)—for mankind, too, is a community. It is not good for man to be alone (Gen. 2:18) precisely because it is not good for God either.

19

The second implication is that we must revise our ideas about the divine *simplicity*. Burrell[5] may be right that for Aquinas this and the other divine attributes were not meant as attributes of God but rather as grammatical rules for speaking about God: thus, to say God is "simple" is to say that human language, structured as it is along composite lines, cannot really say what God is like. However, it is clear that, by and large, Christian thought has regarded the attributes as attributes, and "simplicity" as a straight-forward statement that there is no metaphysical composition in God. If God is a network of interpersonal relationships, then the divinity cannot lack metaphysical composition. Far from being a defect, metaphysical composition must be the very stuff of Being itself, that which makes Being the satisfying thing it is. Scholasticism struggled valiantly to reconcile the traditional idea of the divine simplicity with belief in a trinity, but I think that it failed ultimately. Of course, not all that was being said in the doctrine of God's simplicity need be jettisoned. The composition involved is not the bringing together of separable entities. Moreover, one could argue that the metaphysical components of absolute Being share in the characteristics of such Being and therefore transcend the limitations of our language, based as it is not simply on compositeness but on limitation.

Thirdly, we must revise our ideas about the divine *omnipotence*. It is commonplace in theology to point out that the all-powerful God is *also* a loving God. However, such a statement pictures God's power and love as two distinct entities, with the latter keeping the former within some acceptable sort of check. But if one asserts that love is God's essence, then the only power God has is the power of love. This in turn means that all God's actions must reflect the structures of love. As Geddes MacGregor has pointed out, love is essentially kenotic.[6] This is why "a man can have no greater love than to lay down his life for his friends" (John 15:13). Divine power must therefore consist in the ability to give of oneself, to share oneself. Christians see the ultimate manifestation of this in the crucifixion, an event that John saw as revelatory of Jesus' divine glory (John 17:1).

God's omnipotence is therefore the power of love to give of itself endlessly. Another essential characteristic of love is its respect for the individuality of the individual. This is the first of

Williams's essential categories of love.[7] This theme also under-lies MacGregor's entire approach. To say that love is kenotic means for him not only that love empties itself, but also that it abdicates power. Love's essential characteristic is therefore to "let be," to allow things to be what they will. This is a self-sacrificial power which, in fact, causes God pain. While MacGregor's God is a bit too passive (love can pursue its object with a passionate persistence), he is nevertheless correct in stressing the respect God must have for creation. This in turn implies certain limitations on the divine omnipotence as traditionally conceived, though to state those limitations is not easy.

As regards matter, MacGregor's viewpoint *nisi fallor* would be that God simply lets evolution take its course. In that case one must see its tortuous path with its recurrent dog-eat-dog motif as being *the* testimony to God's nature as love. But this I find unconvincing. If man sees it as loving to actively create conditions in which animal suffering is minimized, why should God's love not do so? A possibly more convincing approach would be to argue that as a reflection of love, matter inevitably displays its kenotic structure. The interchange of energy at the heart of matter is a primitive form of love. It is the physical origin of man's experience of giving. The dying that exists in order that others may live can also be seen as a created reflection of love. As for the resistance to this dying that is only too evident in living creatures, could one not see in this the inevitable deficiencies in created expressions of love, deficiencies that may flow from finite being's understandable fear of letting go of itself? Finitude may well have a built-in instinct of its lack of Being. Perhaps this fear can only be overcome through a long and arduous learning process. Perhaps there is a cosmic dimension to Paul's view of the Law as a pedagogue. But all this is speculation. Its main point is to suggest that the kenotic structure of the divine Being is limited in the sense that God could not create a world structured on non-kenotic lines.

As regards man's freedom, the picture is a trifle clearer. If God is truly love, then he cannot force man to do what he does not want to do. But all have always agreed with this. The traditional problem was that as the creator of freedom, can God not make us *want* to do what we would otherwise not have wanted to do? We are today faced with the possibility that it is not just God who will

21

be able to do that. Sophisticated techniques of behavioral control and alteration are already on our doorstep. The ethical issues are immense. But throughout any discussion of them the issue of respect for freedom still is a basic ethical norm.[8] The fact that we can distinguish between respecting freedom and yet modifying or even genetically prejudicing favorably human behavior indicates that the apparent contradiction between God moving us yet freely is not necessarily as much of a contradiction as many thought. Nevertheless, it remains true that any form of intervention in the psyche of another can only be justified to the extent that it frees the individual's freedom. This implies ultimately that a person retains the real ability to either consent to or refuse something. Applied to our relationship with God, it implies the ability to either love God or refuse to do so. If God is love, then respect for our freedom must ultimately mean that God runs the risk of our refusal to love in return. The doctrine of hell is but the assertion that we *can* refuse to love. It is, paradoxically, an inescapable conclusion if we hold God is love.

All this implies that traditional Christian ideas of predestination must be reexamined. Above all it implies that the idea that God chooses some rather than others to be saved from the *massa damnata* is a blasphemous refusal to take seriously the fact that love "wills the salvation of all men" (1 Tim. 2:4).

But what then of the divine sovereignty? As Sontag reminds us, "omnipotence" is rather an important part of the concept "God."[9] Does all that we have said imply that there is nothing God can really do? If God respects creation, are we not faced with a God whose activity is limited to holding the stage up so that the actors can do what they will? One needs to correct the above picture by reminding ourselves that love is something very active. It has a causal dimension.[10] Why deny to God the passionate persistence we admire in human lovers? God's pursuit of us could well be a very active one—Christians believe it was. How God combines respect for individuality with active pursuit is something I cannot fathom out. We can get some idea as regards God's respect for human freedom—even a human lover knows how to pursue the loved one while respecting freedom. But what it means as regards God's relationship to the material universe, I do not know. Perhaps we simply have to say that a truly active love relationship can

22

only begin even on God's part once creation is able to make that conscious response that we call love.

Fourthly, "God is love" also affects our views of divine *omniscience*. If God is love, then each omniscience is the power of love to know everything about the beloved. As Rahner once put it so beautifully, "love is the lamp of knowledge."[11] He made this observation in connection with the contingency of creation. A creation that is the result of a free choice can have no explanation for its existence other than love. Conversely, one can only know it fully, and not just superficially, by the same attitude that brought it into existence: love. Indeed, all knowledge is a form of love in that it is some sort of drive for unity with an object. And all love is a form of knowledge. The distinction between the two is sufficiently blurred even in our experience for us to have no great difficulty in saying that on the absolute level of being that we call God, knowledge and love are quite indistinguishable. This unity of knowledge and love means that God's love is never irrational or blind. However, it also means that God's knowledge is not the impersonal knowledge of the computer, one that remains unmoved by all it knows. Does the equation of divinity and love throw any light on the knowledge of future free acts traditionally ascribed to God? Because of the complexity of the issues involved, I would not like to say that God does not know future free acts. I realize that actually to hold such a belief raises mind-boggling problems, but a bit of boggling is necessary now and then. The traditional philosophical reason for this is that as the source of being of such acts God must be present to them, and must experience all reality as eternally present to him. The obvious place to attack such an argument is the assertion that God experiences all reality as eternally present. I can concede that God escapes the temporal limitations that we experience. But I see no reason for not asserting that just as the creation of free individuals entails respecting their individuality and freedom, so too the creation of temporal beings entails God's respecting their temporality. This would mean that God *as related to me at this moment* cannot from that relationship know with infallible certainty what I will do tomorrow. God can only do that in and through the relationship we will have tomorrow, even if God does not experience the gap between those events that I do. If God is love, then divine knowledge of my free actions can only come from the actions—not from any sort of *premotio physica* (preordaining—though freely!) or gigantic divine computation of probabilities.

Fifthly, the concept of God's *impassibility* requires revision if God is love. Strictly speaking, impassibility means the inability to be acted upon, to be affected by another. Love is not a one-way relationship. If God is love, then the divinity is a reality that can experience being loved. That means being acted upon—or it means nothing. Moreover, a love relationship that respects individuality and freedom will have its response to the individual shaped by the way in which such freedom is exercised. If God does not control our actions, if we are not puppets, then the way in which God responds to us is *dependent* on the way we act. To say God is dependent on anything seems heresy. But to assert that God's activities are in no way influenced by our actions is, amongst other things, to deny so central a Christian belief as the value of prayer, petitionary prayer. It is true that a whole tradition has developed that tries to explain such prayer as a way of aligning one's will to God's, in order to remain faithful to the belief that God cannot be changed. But the real Christian tradition has always been that prayer *evokes* a response from God. The Israelites too had no problems about the possibility of acting on God. Neither did Jesus, who even compared such prayer to a form of nagging that can evoke a response out of exasperation if nothing else (Luke 18:1-5). The *practical* attitude of the entire Judeo-Christian tradition is that God can be acted upon. It is therefore quite astonishing that belief in the divine impassibility could live and flourish and be adhered to so tenaciously, even taking into account the well known explanation that God has eternally decreed that prayer A should have response B, and prayer B response C, etc.

However, impassibility means more than the inability to be acted upon. In today's vocabulary it means the inability to suffer pain. The tradition that God cannot suffer is under increasing attack today,[12] though the idea of God suffering is by no means entirely new. If God is love, then one has to admit the possibility of some sort of suffering in God. Love can surely not be indifferent to the response given it. Even a divine lover, if truly a lover, must surely "feel" the pain of not being loved in return. But, apart from unrequited love, God, if love, can surely not be indifferent to

24

suffering. Christians are repeatedly taught that Jesus is *the* revelation to us of what God is like. If that is so, then he has revealed to us *God's* sorrow that those he loves could not watch one hour with him (Matt. 26:40), *God's* tears at the suffering of Martha and Mary (John 11:36), *God's* anger at the suffering caused by religious hypocrisy (Matt. 23:13). Christians have willingly accepted that Jesus revealed God's *concern* for us, but did not see in Jesus' suffering a revelation of God's suffering. And yet for Christians, the fact that God (meaning thereby the divine person called "the Son") suffered for mankind is at the heart of their faith. But this was effectively anesthetized by affirming that he suffered only in his human nature. Within the divinity he experienced no suffering. Christians also held that the Father experienced no suffering. But if the Father did not pay any personal price in sending us his Son, and if the Son did not really, as a divine person, experience pain, rejection, and crucifixion, then the Christian praise of such great love on God's part is nonsense. The man called Jesus remains admirable, but there is no need to see in what he did any great sign of love on God's part. The entire Judeo-Christian tradition is built around the idea that God has entered into a personal relationship with people. The earlier image for this was covenant. A later, and more forceful one, was that of marriage. It is rather difficult to reconcile Aristotle's unmoved mover with a God that marries. You cannot believe that God enters into a true relationship with others and yet wish to preserve his immunity from reciprocity.

However, such criticisms are well known. More difficult is the task of providing a metaphysical basis that can allow for such experiences within the divinity. MacGregor believes the basis is to be found in Being's very kenotic structure. For him the act of creation itself was a self-emptying, an act of self-limitation on the part of the divine. "To say that the biblical God is love is to say that his creation is an act not of self-expansion but of self-limitation."[13] As such it causes God pain: God suffers in the very act of creating. "In conferring existence on his creatures, God must somehow endure that existence with some reflection of, or some potentiality for, his own self-limiting creativity, with all the anguish inherent in it."[14] Put bluntly, God did not relish the implications of creation, of parting with his untrammeled possession of Being.[15]

I think the kenotic structure of Being is the right path to follow in one's search of a metaphysics of divine suffering. I am not too sure about creation being an anguish for God, though. Perhaps I am still too tied to the idea of the connection between suffering and sin—i.e., between suffering and the absence or limitations of love. Self-emptying can surely be pure joy. Indeed, the kenotic structure of Being surely testifies not to the fact that joy is found in *suffering* but that joy is found in giving, in self-emptying. Emptying oneself enables one to receive all the more fully. That is the structure of Being. It is also the structure of joy. I would therefore see creation as an outburst of joy on God's part, a further, though unnecessary, extension of Being's basic impulse to share: *bonum diffusivum sui* (goodness wishes to spread itself around)! However, the kenotic structure of Being makes it metaphysically *possible* for Being to suffer. For if its structure is the exchange of love, then unreturned love must affect the structure. Even the awareness of unreturned love amongst others could affect the kenotic structure of God's own Being. I suppose I am slipping into the old idea of disharmony here. Sin strikes a discordant note, and all that. But perhaps there is a metaphysical truth in this idea. When the discordance is experienced within one's being, then it becomes a conscious form of suffering. One could argue that, if all finite being is a sharing in infinite Being, if infinite Being penetrates with its supportive creative presence all finite being, then a denial in the latter realm of the laws of kenosis, that is, the laws of love, may well affect the former.

But is there then no truth enshrined in the traditional teaching of God's impassibility? I think there is. It is that God is not at the mercy of passion and pain the way human beings are. Prestige[16] sees this as *the* point patristic thought was making when it stressed the divine impassibility. It is linked to the idea of God's perfect moral freedom.[17] In our terms, the divine impassibility is love's inability to be threatened, to suffer in a way that its character as love is affected. "Impassibility" is a way of asserting that God's Being is perfect, i.e., that God's love cannot be marred by imperfections.

Sixthly, all the foregoing implies a radical change from traditional conceptions of the divine *immutability*. None of what has been said is compatible with the traditional concept of God's immutability. Christians above all must concede that by becoming man the *logos*, the Son, became something other than it was. Rahner has drawn attention to this by pointing out that to say God

26

became man is to assert that God *can* become something different.[18] Rahner tries to honor traditional teaching by saying that God can experience change in something other than the divinity. However, what this means is not clear. It has justly been pointed out many times over that the biblical view of God's immutability refers not to any Greek ideas of inherent metaphysical changelessness but rather to his constancy. If God is love, then divine immutability is the constancy of divine love. Immutability can also mean that God can never become more God or less God—which is to say God can never become more loving or less loving.

The whole issue of divine immutability has been attacked from so many quarters in recent years that one need not labor the matter. However, what could perhaps do with a bit of attention are the philosophical reasons that Christian theologians traditionally appealed to in order to support their belief in God's changelessness. Basically, the objection to any idea of change in God was that change implied imperfection. Change, as Aristotle put it, was a movement from potency to act. As such it implies a state of affairs where the fullness of actualized Being does not yet exist. But if this fullness of Being does not exist already, then there is no hope that it will ever exist, for where then is the reservoir of Being from which to fill the void? To change the terms, God must either be God or there is no God. There is no hope of a non-God ever becoming God. God therefore is pure Act, the changeless one.

Since it is Christian theologians who have appealed to the above argument, a useful critique of it is the following. The very affirmation that beings exist that are not God strikes at the root of the act/potency distinction. As used by Aquinas, that root was the idea that potency indicated an absence of the fullness of Being, hence limitation. But if God is not his creatures, then there is a dimension of being absent from God. Of course, the scholastics were fully aware of this. Their answer was that finite being was a purely derived Being. Absolute Being already contained in itself, therefore, all the perfections to be found in finite being, as their source and ground. However, after all is said and done, the fact remains that the Absolute *can* be the source of being other than itself, without this implying the taint of limitation within itself, without it implying the sort of unrealized potentiality that would be incompatible with the fullness of Being.

But if this is so, then why can the Absolute not be a source of further manifestations of being *within* itself? To repeat the argument in a different way, if the concept "fullness of Being" means the actual realization of all possible forms of existence, then God must be his creatures: a conclusion the scholastics would not admit. If it does not mean that, then there is the possibility of the divinity realizing within itself new forms of existence. One may reply that the concept "fullness of Being" means the actual realization of all possible forms of *Absolute* Being. But then one can ask why it is so defined—is there a reason within Absolute Being itself that demands such a definition?

So much for the outlines of a theological answer (theological because based on the faith conviction of the real distinction between God and his creatures). What about a philosophical response? Here I am out of my depth. However, the way I would go about such a response is as follows. As I see it, the problem has two connected elements. First of all, there is the idea that the fullness of Being could not have any unrealized potentialities, since the inner dynamism of Being is such as not to limit itself in any way (and unrealized potentialities are seen as such a limitation). In scholasticism this argument took the form of the negation of any self-limiting ability to the act part of the act/potency distinction. In reply, I would argue that it is part of the very nature of infinite Being to have an infinitude of potentialities. Infinite Being could never realize all its own potentialities: that would be to contradict itself. It is interesting that for Aristotle and his contemporaries, infinity was associated with the indeterminate, with potency. All actuality, including Pure Act, implied a limit, in the sense that it was a being completely rounded off, so to speak. I suspect that here again cosmological ideas were more influential than realized. Aristotelian cosmology conceived of entities as in either a finished or an unfinished state. Potency existed in entities that were as yet unfinished. To talk therefore of God as having as yet unrealized potentialities is to talk of him as a being in an unfinished state— which seems to me absurd. However, contemporary cosmology enables us to see unlimited potentiality as a perfection rather than the opposite.

The second element of the problem is the need to account for the movement from potency to act. Here the problem is one of a sufficient credit balance of being. Whence the being to allow for such a movement? I see no problem in simply asserting that it is a testimony to the very fullness of the divine Being that it is also able to actualize unlimited potentialities within and for itself. Here again, one must assert that precisely because divinity has the fullness of Being it also has the fullness of becoming. It is the potentialities of creatures that are limited and limiting, because the ultimate ontological source of their actualization is not their own but the divine Being.

J. Y. Lee reminds us that Westerners have for too long been bound to an "either-or" mentality.[19] "If God is ultimate reality he must be ultimate *both* in actuality *and* in potentiality."[20] Lee's view, like that of the process theologians, is diametrically opposed to the traditional one. He holds that God's basic reality is change. This he distinguishes from becoming, which is a form of change. However, he interestingly enough insists on affirming that God is stable too. He sees this insistence on God's basic stability as differentiating his view from the process one.[21] God is therefore, paradoxically, changeless change, a being whose basic, unaltering structure is that of change. "Changelessness is the...constant and regular form of change."[22] I think that Lee's affirmations are not simply clever but ultimately empty paradoxes. They point to a profound truth. Put in other terms, God's basic reality is a dynamism of love that is unalterable in its character as love. Lee is right in warning us against using *simply* the category of change for God. Such a category taken seriously would lead us to the unacceptable affirmation that God is pure potency—which is pure nonbeing. As we have seen, God can have infinite potentialities simply because he is infinite act. The latter—a dynamic reality, not a static situation—is the ground of the former, while the former reveals the nature of the latter. That God is "both-and" is not simply an Eastern tradition, but part of Western thought too. In fact, "both-and" speech is a linguistic homage to the transcendence of the reality we are trying to describe.

Seventhly, and finally, a brief word about God's *unity*. If God is love, then the divine unity is that which is created in and through relationships. The model for it is not the solid atom, but the relativity and ceaseless dying that life may continue that characterizes the whole of reality as we experience and value it.

Implications for Our Experience of God's Activity in the World

Firstly, if God is love, then *the* sign of God's activity or presence in the world is love. In fact, I would say that it is the only sign of his presence. All the well-known signs that have been appealed to—miracles, speaking in tongues, ecstatic experiences, etc.—had revelatory value only to the extent that they revealed either love or the demands or judgments thereof (for love *does* make demands on us, does place us under judgment, even while letting us be). The Apostle Paul was well aware of the limited value of the various phenomena associated with the Spirit's presence. He was aware, for example, that ecstatic utterances were found amongst the pagans. However, what for him made these phenomena a sign of the Spirit's presence was the fact that within the Church they were used to build up the community, which he saw as a work of love.

To say that love is *the* sign of God's presence is to say that wherever there is love, there you have God present. God must not be looked for in the gaps left in our knowledge of reality, but in any and every form of love (and judgment on evil—even violent opposition to evil can be a form of love). One is therefore confronted—joyfully or otherwise—with God wherever one is confronted by love and its demands. When my neighbor loves me, this is a sign to me of God's presence not only to him but also to me: indeed to the two of us in the bond created by that love. Moreover, the reverse is also true: when I love my neighbor I am at one and the same time loving God. By this I do not mean that I am carrying out God's command to love my neighbor and am *thereby* showing love for God. Rather does it mean that the very act of loving a neighbor reaches out, whether the lover realizes it or not, to God? The theologian most famous for this thesis is, of course, Karl Rahner,[23] who argues that the transcendental condition for any human love is a reaching out (in love) for the infinite, just as the transcendental condition for any knowledge of the world around us is an unreflected *Vorgriff* (a pre-grasping) of infinite reality.[24]

The Catholic tradition within Christianity has preserved an important insight in its insistence on the sacramental character of marriage. For marriage is *the* finite, human expression of God's own nature. The Eucharist may and does express people's unity with the historical form that God's own marriage with humanity took. But marriage expresses something more primordial still: God's own inner nature. There is, for Christians, much food for thought in the reflection that the unity of man and wife in one flesh reflects the unity of Father and Son in one Spirit.

Secondly, if *the* sign of God in the world is love, then this, I believe, can serve as a way for evaluating various claims to God's revelation. This is one of the reasons why I personally remain convinced that in the Judeo-Christian tradition we have a genuine revelation of God. Indeed, it is why I believe that that revelation has a fullness about it that enables it to serve as a criterion for evaluating other claims to revelation. I hope others are no more offended by such convictions about my tradition than I am by their views or even by their negative judgments regarding such convictions. But what for me is of supreme significance in the Judeo-Christian tradition (which of course is more than just Christianity) is the fact that it presents the God it believes in as one who actively seeks a love relationship with people. This love relationship is already adumbrated in the covenant image, where love of God and love of neighbor are a central part of the contract. The relationship is expressed in various ways, as time goes on, none more touching surely than: "Does a woman forget her baby at the breast, or fail to cherish the son of her womb? Yet even if these forget, I will never forget you" (Isa. 49:15). However, with the prophets Hosea and especially Ezekiel God's relationship with the Israelites is explicitly conceived of in marital terms (see, e.g., Ezek. 16). Paul applied this imagery to the relationship between Christ, the incarnate Lord, and his Church, the new people of God (Eph. 5:31-32). The culminating insight of this whole tradition into God's nature is expressed in the text that forms the theme of this paper: "God is love" (1 John 4:8).

In the Judeo-Christian tradition, then, (and as far as I know in it alone) God is conceived of as one who actively seeks a love relationship with humanity. So actively does he seek it that he is presented as having become one with mankind, and even dying for its sake. This is why I see in that tradition a supreme example of divine revelation.

Finally, I would like to say something about the implications of "God is love" for the way in which Christian beliefs in salvation should be understood.[25] Christianity has always held that we have

31

been saved by Jesus' death (and also his incarnation, life, and resurrection—but I wish to focus here simply on his death). However, there has never been any unanimity as to the way in which his death achieved this. The New Testament uses several images to illustrate in a graphic way the fact that that death was salvific—ransom, sacrifice, victory, merit, to name the most significant ones. However, in post-apostolic times first the concept of vicarious satisfaction and then that of vicarious punishment appeared on the scene, the former being beloved to Catholics, the latter to Protestants. The former operates, whether it realizes it or not, with an image of God as the victim of the divine celestial judicial system: infinite dishonor must be repaid with infinite honor. The latter concept (vicarious punishment) operates with a perhaps even worse image: the tyrant who demands his pound of flesh before being willing to forgive. Both theories contradict Jesus' view of God. Nowhere does Jesus give the impression that his Father needs placating before being willing to forgive the world or that he is unable to do so before certain wrongs to the divinity are righted. On the contrary, he simply preached the unconditional forgiveness of God. It is worth remembering that he did so before his death—without issuing promissory notes of forgiveness redeemable only after that day. In other words, both theories contradict God's essential nature as love. If God is love, then God's redeeming activity must be manifested in love. Objective salvation (i.e., the event that makes salvation a real possibility for individuals) must be something achieved by love, and not by restoring honor or enduring punishment.

To present a coherent picture of a salvation achieved purely by love one has to begin with some idea of God's purpose in creating. If God is love, his purpose could surely be none other than enablement of other beings to experience love. In other words, God's purpose must have been the establishment of a community of love. Christianity believes that such was the case and that such a community was meant to exist not only between human beings but also between them and the community that is God. God's final aim was the establishment of a "God-mankind" community. Hence the incarnation and the indwelling of the Spirit. The constancy of God's love (immutability) means that nothing could deflect God from that purpose. The old idea of God having to go back to the drawing board after man sinned is unacceptable. What is true is that the presence of evil (however explained) meant that God's intended unity with mankind would inevitably involve the divinity sharing in suffering. Salvation consists in the fact that God did not shrink from this but accepted it.

Jesus' attitude to the social and religious outcasts of his time aroused the opposition of many. When analyzed, the point at issue was precisely one of love: the *theological* issue was whether love of neighbor was as important as love of God; the *existential* issue, one that made it as difficult for many Pharisees of the time to agree with Jesus' views as it is for many white South Africans to draw the correct conclusions from them today, was the threat to their position contained in truly loving the "rabble" (as they saw them). The only way Jesus could have avoided death was by withdrawing his love from the outcasts—i.e., by siding with his enemies' views regarding God and God's judgment on such people. However, Jesus—the incarnation of one of the lovefilled relationships within the divinity—died rather than do that. He died rather than withdraw his love. The result, Christians believe, is that he and his love are with us now forever. The unity between God and mankind begun in the incarnation and for which Jesus died, is now a permanent feature of our universe: something that has many theological implications, especially for that curious thing called the state of "original sin."

Conclusion

When taken seriously, the affirmation that God is love can revolutionize our ideas about the divinity. I do not think it can provide final solutions to the age-old problems about freedom and the divine concursus, evil, etc. To "solve" any such questions involves laying all the ingredients before our eyes—and we cannot do that to that dimension of Being that is the source of our own existence. However, the characterization of God as love does, I submit, make God a far more meaningful reality as well as give us a deeper insight into the aforementioned issues.

NOTES

1 See, e.g., E. Jüngel, *Gott als Geheimnis der Welt* (Tübingen: Mohr, 1977); G. W. Newland, *Theology of the Love of God* (London: Collins, 1980); D. D. Williams, *The Spirit and Forms of Love* (Washington, D.C.: The University Press of America, 1981); G. MacGregor, *He Who Lets Us Be* (New York: Seabury, 1975).

2 C. Bittle, *God and His Creatures* (Milwaukee, Wisc.: Bruce, 1953), 199 (a good example of popularized neo-scholasticism).

3 Cf. Bittle, 201.

4 C. H. Dodd, *The Johannine Epistles* (London: Hodder & Stoughton, 1953), 109.

5 D. Burrell, *Aquinas: God and Action* (London: Routledge & Kegan Paul, 1979).

6 MacGregor.

7 D. D. Williams, 114ff.

8 Cf. B. Häring, *Manipulation* (Slough: St. Paul, 1975), 57ff.

9 Frederick Sontag, "Love and Freedom," *Encounter* 43 (1982): 255.

10 Williams, 118ff.

11 K. Rahner, *Hearers of the Word* (London: Sheed and Ward, 1969), 100.

12 See, e.g., Moltmann, *The Crucified God* (London: SCM Press, 1974), chap. 6; H. Urs von Balthasar, "Le Mystère Pascal," in *Mysterium Salutis*, tome 3, vol. 12 (Paris: Éditions du Cerf, 1972); K. Kitamori, *Theology of the Pain of God* (London: SCM Press, 1966); and MacGregor and Jüngel, as well as representatives of the school of Process theology.

13 MacGregor, 19.

14 Ibid.

15 Ibid., 106.

16 G. L. Prestige, *God In Patristic Thought* (London: SPCK, 1952), 6-7.

17 Ibid.

18 K. Rahner, "On the theology of the Incarnation," in *Theological Investigations* (London: Darton, Longman & Todd, 1966), 4:112ff.

19 See J. Y. Lee, *The Theology of Change* (New York: Maryknoll, 1979), 16-17.

20 Ibid., 18.

21 Ibid., 18-19.

22 Ibid., 44.

23 See K. Rahner, "Reflections on the unity of the love of neighbour and the love of God," in *Theological Investigations*, 6:231ff.

24 See his seminal works, K. Rahner, *Spirit in the World* (London: Sheed and Ward, 1968) and *Hearers of the Word.*

25 See my article "How are we Saved?," in *Theologica Evangelica* (Journal of the Faculty of Theology, University of South Africa) 12, nos. 2 & 3 (1979): 49-55.

The Divine Historicity

Galen A. Johnson

There is a passage in Soren Kierkegaard's *Philosophical Fragments* that is worth hearing, not for the completely standard position it states, but for the question it raises. In the "Interlude," Kierkegaard took the trouble to make the following declaration: "It is the perfection of the Eternal to have no history, and of all that is, the Eternal alone has absolutely no history."[1] This very denial calls attention to a question about divine Being that must be raised in our age, an age in which historicity has moved into the center of how we philosophize about the meaning of being a person. If the concept of "person" is to be taken seriously philosophically as the central symbol for understanding the Being of God, must we not be willing to speak of the historicity of God? For incarnational religions such as Christianity that claim a divine identity for a human being who lived in history, the question is intensified.

In this essay, I shall attempt to think as deeply as I am able the meaning of divine personhood in terms of historicity. To do so, we shall need to clarify (1) what is meant by an historical existence, (2) the structure of an ontology of historicity, and (3) the compatibility of such an ontology with the divine Being. My hope in this age of historical consciousness, is to mitigate one of the new paradoxes in the idea of God as person, the paradox that God the eternal is historical in himself. Our thought will be aided by that philosopher with whom Kierkegaard's views are nearly always to be contrasted, Georg Hegel, who wrote in *The Philosophy of History* of the "infinite and eternal history of God."[2]

Human Being as Historical Being

The movement of historicity to the front and center of philosophical thought about personhood leaps from the pages of Heidegger's *Being and Time,* as well as from Merleau-Ponty's *Phenomenology of Perception.* Yet the centrality of historicity is broader than the existentialists, typical also of Hegel, Marx, Dilthey, Whitehead, Husserl, Croce, Collingwood, and Dewey. An *historical existence* is one in which past acts are cumulatively retained and future acts anticipated in presence, such that description of the meaning of a present action presupposes description of the relevant past and future. Human experience, actions included, cannot be atomized into simple, discrete temporal bits of homogeneous linear duration, a "present" in clock-time. *Presence* has a thickness to it because human action is not another thing in the world to be observed but a network of meanings lived out by a subject who is never object. The same arm motion, scientifically observed as a succession of discrete positions by a body in space and time, could be in living experience a greeting, the end of a friendship, the beginning of a day on the stock exchange, the beginning of a war. It depends upon the relevant past and future sedimented and anticipated in the action. What is in presence for a person can be a moment, a day, a year, even a life,[3] for the raising of an arm is also, and ultimately, a person dying. Human being in presence has a temporally complex structure that conditions what presence means.

If a human action is temporally complex, to describe it as occurring at a certain time entails that certain other events must have occurred at other times. One cannot introduce a father or wife or display a battle scar or read Hegel's second book without the occurrence of relevant earlier events. The difference between an historical and a nonhistorical existent is the difference between action that is irreducibly temporally complex and event that occurs in a simple and discrete present moment. Human presence is both past and future referring, and to know what a human action *is* requires describing it in the light of that certain past and future.

It is often thought that the paradox that God the eternal is historical is the paradox that the unchanging eternal is temporal. In truth, the apparent offense to thinking is even deeper, for an historical existence is not sheerly a temporal existence, but a certain form of temporal existence. If this were not true, historicity would fail to distinguish human being from natural being, for nature also is a temporal, changing succession of states. Meteors rise in the heavens and fall, the ocean tides move in and out, mountains jut forth and are worn down, the seasons come and go, all in a temporal rhythm. There is a paradox of eternity and temporal succession in the divine Being to the extent that God is creator, sustainer, or otherwise involved with the natural order. However, this paradox is not the same as that of God as historical, for historicity denotes a quality of temporal *presence*. Genuine historicity can only be attributed mistakenly to a purely natural event, for temporal complexity is not constitutive of natural occurrences. Natural events can be given atemporal descriptions, as exhibited by their capacity for natural scientific mathematization. Changes in mountains and ocean plates, for example, although optionally describable as complex events, as we sometimes speak of a "new" break or mountain, may also be described without loss in the non-referring vocabulary of linear dating, "and then, and then, and then." To establish a history, events must have a temporally layered referential character, one event standing as the visible surface of other events sedimented in it. Of course, we could have a history of a natural object relative to its role in human affairs, but split off from such human vantage points, natural objects and events lack the referential structure necessary for a history.[4]

We are all aware that the word "history" has been appropriated for descriptions of the development of natural objects in natural sciences such as paleontology and evolutionary biology. We need not quarrel over a word, for there is an important conceptual difference between synchronic and diachronic sciences. However, univocal linguistic usage should not lead us into a failure of philosophical conception, the failure to distinguish between existents such as rocks that change from one temporal state to another, and persons, whose presence cumulatively retains and refers to its past and anticipates its future. The human succession in time is not simply a succession, but a history because human beings

39

stand at the intersection of the past and future, and referentially take up both in their living presence.[5] Such referential preservation and anticipation is inseparable from the very essence of persons.

It will be worth our time in a moment, when we begin to test the compatibility of historical concepts and the Being of God, if I take the trouble at this juncture to include a word about narrative description. The linguistic form that is best suited to characterizing an action in a way that captures the complex temporal ordering relations constitutive of it is narrative description. By a narrative I mean a description correlative to complex human action, a description of what a present action is in the light of the earlier and later actions sedimented in it.[6] For example, consider Kaufmann's narrative description of Hegel's philosophical work: "Hegel...tried to do from a Protestant point of view what Aquinas had attempted 600 years earlier: he sought to fashion a synthesis of Greek philosophy and Christianity."[7] The description is narrative, not because it is stated in the past tense, but because it describes Hegel's philosophical project, 1797-1831, in the light of Aquinas's earlier project. More simple cases of narration are these: "The player struck out and lost the game," "Here is my father," or "The next war will be the last war." A narrative is not an annal or chronicle that lists one event after another in sequence of succession. It is a description appropriate to the temporal complexity of human action, in which the past and future referentially imbedded in an action are employed to describe the present.

If human life itself is historical, our understanding of it is wedded to correct narrative descriptions of the actions of persons, who are above all historical beings. However, there is a structural incompleteness in the human situation that limits our ability to narrate human affairs. In narrative description, a present is described in the light of past and future actions. Yet both past and future that disclose the meaning of an action are indefinitely open. From the temporal standpoint of the agent who performs it as well as the historian who subsequently describes it, the meaning of the action is therefore ongoing and underdetermined. From the prospective temporal perspective of the agent who acts, what the action is depends upon the past accumulated in it and the plans, intentions, and hopes that structure it. But the meaning of those past actions referred to includes the past references in them, the past in that past, and thus we are pushed further back in history attempting to fix the temporal context that will in turn fix the meaning of the action. On the side of the future anticipated, plans and intentions are only possibilities, not actualities established in the web of human relationships, and what is done as an act of liberation or peace may in fact become an act of utmost enslavement or violence. Moreover, the future-referring side of human action also presents a structural limit on the historian's retrospective description. An historian describing the nineteenth century from a position in the twentieth may well know that Hegel's philosophy was the beginning of existentialism and Marxism, a description that would astonish Hegel, but the twentieth-century historian is, of course, unable to describe the nineteenth century from a position in the twenty-first century.

Many thinkers have infelicitously allowed the concept of narrative to merge with that of story,[8] and popular usage certainly condones such an identification. However, if we understand by story its classic Aristotelian sense (*mūthos*),[9] we must resist this identification, for a story is the emplotment of action over time to display its beginning, middle, and end. Our narrative understanding is always stuck in the middle, structurally limited, with the beginning and end of action implicated but always enshrouded. The openness within the meaning of historical existence is part and parcel of every human presence, and would come to rest only in the first moment of history with no historical future extending beyond it. Historical understanding lives in between myths of creation and apocalypse, and the secular never outruns but always invokes the train of the sacred.

An Ontology of Historical Being

With the concepts of historical existence and narrative description available, we are not quite yet in a position to test the possibility of conceiving God as historical being. We need to find out more about the ontology of the being who is historical, for although historicity explicitly denotes a certain quality of temporal presence, it implies a network of closely clustered concepts about self, social relations, and situation. After this ontology is more fully available we can see whether it is compatible with the Being of God worshipped in religious life. The non-substantialist ontology of historical being we seek will be illuminated by implicit guidance from the philosophical book that has taken historicity more seriously than any other, Hegel's *Phenomenology of Spirit,* in particular its fourth chapter on self-consciousness and its sixth on the history of Spirit.[10]

If persons are centrally historical existents, not sheerly temporally sequential as in the case of natural objects, but living presences in which past is preserved and future anticipated, what we *are* in presence is constituted out of what our past has been and what our future is anticipated to be. Historicity means that humans do not have some permanent nature with capacities to act in certain prescribed ways, but our acting becomes our "nature." We must be careful in stating such an ontological perspective, for no individual by his actions makes himself from scratch, and there are genuine metaphysical quandaries about why historical presence develops reliably in a person and not in a cat or canary. Some structural "ability" or "potential" to become historical seems to be presupposed as given within the constitution of persons that is absent in nonpersons. More attention will be given to such qualifications as we move forward. Nevertheless, the starting point for the ontology of historical being is that we are what we do because what we do remains sedimented in our presence, and we should not mistake what is a determinate historical product for a permanent prefashioned essence. Ontologically, historicity most primitively means that:

(1) Persons are self-constituting or self-making beings.

I believe this point can be put in the more popular form that persons are always subjects, never objects. A subject is one who is only partly determinate and describable, in this case because past is preserved in presence, but who always surpasses the determinations of what the past has been. A person is named and addressed, never exhaustively described and objectified. Persons, in other words, are surpassing freedom.

There is an apparent logical absurdity in the notion of self-making, however, for in order to think it through, we find ourselves positing a substantial self who then makes itself. But if there is a substantial self originally needed to make the self, then the idea of self-making is a ruse. The dilemma is humorously expressed by Emil Fackenheim's repetition of a story of Schopenhauer's: the doctrine is "no less absurd than the story of Baron von Muenchhausen, who claimed that, having fallen into a swamp, he pulled himself out by his hair."[11] Or one thinks of the famous Escher impossibility drawing of two hands, each drawing the other. The only way for the idea of self-making to be cogent logically is if self-making is indirect, established over against an otherness that mediates selfhood. Persons do not make themselves directly or immediately, a logical absurdity, but make a world and in so making, make themselves. Self-making is secondary, mediated by and derivative from world-making. Thus, to our originating onto-logical doctrine, another must be added:

(2) Persons make a world that is not-self, and in so making, establish themselves by surpassing or transcending that world.

The exact nature of the otherness that mediates self-making is also critical, for the surpassing of otherness that establishes the self will yet be influenced and formed by that otherness. The world that is made as an other will enter into who the self becomes; the self will be "in the image" of the other it makes but surpasses. Therefore, the most decisive otherness from which self is derivative must be another self who is also a self-making. The reason is clear enough: if a person establishes himself through the surpassing of natural artifacts he makes employing materials from the natural habitat, he inevitably incorporates the preestablished essentialist limits within natural being into his own becoming. Thus, historical being gradually would be replaced by natural being. It is only another person who is both not-self and yet does not have natural, essentialist limits that contradict the histori-cality of self-making. Thus, to our second doctrine, we should add a third:

(3) Persons make a world of relations to other persons who are not-self, and in so making, establish themselves by surpassing those relations.

Finally, we see that implicit in the formulation of this third feature of the ontological structure of historical existence is a fourth, detectable in the change from "making the other" *per se*, to "making *relations* with" an other self. As we noted at the outset, this fourth feature was indeed already implicit in the very notions of world-making and self-making from the beginning, for human world-making always confronts an other, whether natural or human, that it did not originate. No human being makes the world of artifacts, or more decisively the world of human relations *ex nihilo,* but makes them on the basis of what the natural and human orders already are. Making worldly artifacts is conditioned and limited by the prefixed essences of natural being, and making human relations is conditioned and limited by the social determinate past, preserved within the presence of other persons as well as within social institutions handed down. The past of a human presence is finite, for we are all born at a certain place and time, as is the future finite, for we are all destined to die at a place and time. Such is our *natural situation.* Moreover, we act toward others on the basis of languages, tools, and institutions of work and power that we receive and do not make. Such is our *historical situation.* The freedom of world-making and self-making is limited by the thrownness and destiny of natural and historical situation, and this is just what we mean by finitude. Therefore,

(4) *Persons make a world of artifacts and human relations, and make themselves by surpassing that world, but all within the limits of natural and historical situation.*

As our most profound philosophers have understood, the relationship of freedom and fate is truly dialectical; for we do make the world and ourselves, but we do not make them absolutely as we choose. Self-making, world-making, social relatedness, and situation, each of these deserves much more reflection, but they are the bare ontological pillars that support the concept of historical existence.

The History of God and the Divine as Person

We are now able to turn our attention to the inquiry into whether it makes religious and theological sense to map an ontology of historical being onto the divine reality.

In every philosophical epoch, I am convinced, conceptualizing divine Being will present paradoxes; but I am also convinced that the precise shape of the paradoxes will differ, for what is philosophically plausible and possible differs. In the fifth century A.D., for example, the central paradox in thinking of God as person took the form of the apparent impossibility of two irreconcilable and contradictory forms being instantiated in one existent. In our post-Hegelian age, philosophical questioning is permeated

44

by an historical consciousness that it is easy to show the Greek philosophers did not even imagine.[12] Plato certainly did not. Thus, the contemporary paradox of God as person has a different shape, formed around a nonessentialist notion of person as historical existence. Whereas the Platonic essentialist metaphysic generated the paradox of the unity of two incompatible essences, the contemporary metaphysic of historicality generates the paradox of historical situation and historical transcendence. In light of such changed philosophical plausibilities, our effort would be to test the unity of the traditional symbol of "person" with modern historical consciousness.[13] It was with such thoughts in mind that Karl Barth wrote in his *Church Dogmatics,* "we must be careful not to form pagan conceptions of God and the eternal life that He lives and the eternal life that He promises to man, as though at bottom God was a supreme being with neither life, nor activity, nor history... *God is historical even in Himself,* and much more so in His relationship to the reality which is distinct from Himself."[14]

From within the Jewish and Christian religious traditions, two persistent clues have not been suppressed by the substantialist ontological tradition. The first is that both the Hebrew and Christian scriptures are taken up in large measure with the narrative of God's acts in history, narrative descriptions that at least in the case of persons are the linguistic form correlative to the temporal complexity of historical existence. Above all, God is a doer, and to take what the verbs signify out of God's nature would gut Hebrew and Christian scripture. The second clue is the etymology of the Greek name for God employed in the New Testament. The name *theos* derives from either of two verbs, *theoreo* (i.e., I see) or *theo* (i.e., I run), or probably from both. "As it is written," John Scotus Erigena quoted Psalm 147:16 in this hermeneutic context, "Swiftly runs his Word." The New Testament name of God is justly interpreted in the form of verbs, the one who sees and runs through all. Erigena comments: "Hence the two interpretations of the name 'God' are to be understood in a single sense. For his running through all things is nothing else than seeing all things, even as it is through his seeing and flowing through all things that they come to exist through him."[15] We shall return to Erigena's thought, for his *On The Division of Nature* is one of the earliest texts in Christendom (9th century) that speaks of the "history" of God.

Such clues are convincing enough that the idea of God as historical ought to be taken more seriously than it has been, at least within the Jewish and Christian theological traditions. To give it fuller consideration, however, a philosophical inquiry is required that has both a formal and a material dimension; the formal, whether the four ontological features enumerated for historical being require modification or elimination in the case of God, and the material, whether the Being of God can be displayed as self-making mediated by otherness. I am not about to attempt completion of such a formidable task in this essay. Rather I will engage in some comments on the formal side of the problematic, and illustrate one case of the material side from Hegel's interpretation of Christian theology, in order to arrive at what I think one should (and should not) mean when he speaks of the Divine as person.

On the formal side, what is perhaps most surprising about the ontology of historical existence is its eminent suitability for articulating much of what the nature of the Divine must be, not its unsuitability. It is an ontology of creative world-making, of surpassing freedom, of self-other relatedness, and of immanence and transcendence. The most important qualifications center around the doctrines of natural and historical situation, for as eternal, God was not born and will not die, thus is not confronted with a natural situation of finitude. Moreover, the notion of historical situation needs some recasting in the case of God, although not elimination, for any determinate past that is a limit on God's presence, even if it is a past preserved in the worldly otherness God has made, is a *self*-limitation freely undertaken and not a limitation into which God has been thrown as are we. Our past is finite, thus is our freedom qualified; as eternal, God's past is infinite, thus is his freedom self-qualified. In the case of eternal God, therefore, we are required to replace the human natural and historical situations that limit self-making with a conception of the *divine situation,* in which possibilities, once actualized, remain as freely undertaken self-limitations preserved in God's eternal presence.

Charles Hartshorne's essay on the divine historicity is very helpful on the point of unifying historicity and divine perfection. What must be denied in the case of the historicity of God, Hartshorne argues, is past and future in the deficient, finite forms found in human life. "The past as much more largely forgotten than remembered, the future as poorly understood, or as cause of fretful anxiety, also the past as extending back of one's own birth, or the future as extending beyond one's own death—these and related deficiencies are not divine." But, Hartshorne adds, "it is faulty analysis which identifies past and future as such with these deficiencies."[16]

This essay has shown, therefore, that the view from Kierkegaard's *Philosophical Fragments* cited at the outset is incorrect on two counts. Recall Kierkegaard's statement: "It is the perfection of the Eternal to have no history, and of all that is, the Eternal alone has absolutely no history." However, we have seen that it is a mistake to believe that nature has a genuine history, and on the point of perfection, it is not the case that historicity is necessarily an imperfection. Historicity denotes a quality of temporal presence that in the ontology of human persons is united with the limitations of historical and natural situation, and in the ontology of the Divine as person is united with self-limitations and perfection of divine situation.

To leave room for this difference between the ontology of historical being and the divine reality that lives without natural or historical situation, let us say, in the mode of John Scotus Erigena's affirmative *and* negative theology,[17] that God is not historical *per se,* but God is *superhistorical.* God is historical— affirmation; God is not historical—negation; God is superhistorical—affirmation and negation. Similarly, because God is superhistorical, he is both being, as the ontological majority tradition has held, and not-being, as the minority meontological tradition argued.[18] He is being inasmuch as he has actualized certain possibilities among others in world-making and self-making that are preserved in his eternal presence, but not-being inasmuch as God is not simply another being in the world and inasmuch as his world-making and self-making have a surpassing fulfillment yet to be actualized. God is historical and not-historical, being and not-being, universality and particularity, for God must be on both sides of such abstractions. Only so can he be more than a mere abstraction, one who is always subject and never object. Part of Hegel's genius in the *Phenomenology* is his steady hold on both the necessary universality and particularity of reality, from the earliest forms of sense-consciousness, "this" and "that," "here" and "now,"

47

through the forms of self-consciousness, "I," to the forms of Spirit. It is the "divine nature" of language, he argues, to foil all attempts at bifurcating the dialectical relation between universality and particularity.[19] For Hegel, the incarnation of God in Jesus was the culminating picture (*Vorstellung*) of Spirit, the universal that is particular and the particular that is universal.

The material side of testing the compatibility of historical being and divine reality will vary depending upon the specific content of how God is understood in varying religious and theological traditions. Thus, the material issue of the descriptive content of how God is historical is a case by case study. Since the reference point for the ontology of historical being developed here has been Hegel's philosophical history of Spirit, let me limit my comments on the material side of the inquiry to Hegel's interpretation of Christian theology. This will provide an example of the gains, and losses, to be garnered from thinking of God as historical in himself. It will also allow me to put some distance between Hegel and myself.

I regard Hegel's way of unifying the being of God with the world-making and self-making ontology of historical existence as seriously flawed. As I have already indicated, there is no philosopher, in my judgment, who has better understood the ontology of historical existence and its logic. However, Hegel synthesized Christian theology with that ontology of historicity as a dialectical alienation within the Trinity of Father, Son, and Holy Spirit. God the Father, being-in-itself who is the creator of the natural order, has his otherness in the Son, being-for-itself who is Jesus born and crucified, establishing the truth of divine identity as the Spirit, being-in-and-for-itself who is the history of art, religion, and philosophy. This is the infinite history of God, Hegel tells us, a dialectical movement from the self-diremption of Father and Son to self-reconciling Spirit: "Christ—man as man—in whom unity of God and man has appeared, has in his death, and his history generally, himself presented the *eternal history of God.*"[20]

As we know, there is both a left-wing and a right-wing way to interpret the Hegelian history of God. Hegel himself increasingly attempted to pull interpreters toward the right wing as he continued to lecture in Berlin until 1831. In his lectures on the philosophy of history, for example, Hegel discussed the incarnation of God as Jesus in these terms: "The appearance of the Christian God involves further its being unique in its kind; it can occur only once, for God is realized as Subject, and as manifested Subjectivity is exclusively One Individual."[21] Other than such late texts, the strongest evidence in favor of right-wing interpretation is a logical, not historical, reading of the relation among Father, Son, and Holy Spirit, in which God the Father is dialectically transformed but preserved in the Son who is dialectically transformed but preserved in the Spirit. Then, however, we are left wondering how to understand this logical pattern as the "infinite *history* of God." Looking back on the nineteenth century, it was certainly the left-wing reading of Hegel by the Young Hegelians, especially Strauss and Feuerbach, that gained predominance. For them, Jesus was a human moment in the history of God who displayed for the first time the potential all persons have to become sons of God. There is, for example, this text in the *Phenomenology of Spirit,* to counter the right wing and support the left, in which Hegel discusses the true relation of the individual unhappy consciousness to the "incarnate Unchangeable":

> The Unhappy Consciousnesss...knows the Unchangeable itself essentially as an individuality. But what it does *not* know is that this its object, the Unchangeable, which it knows essentially in the form of individuality, is its *own* self, is itself the individuality of consciousness.[22]

It is possible to trace such passages right on through the later Berlin period of Hegel's thought. For example, in the lectures on philosophy of religion, Hegel interprets the universal meaning of the crucifixion of Jesus:

> "God himself is dead," as it is said in a Lutheran hymn; the consciousness of this fact expresses the truth that the human, the finite, frailty, weakness, the negative, is itself a divine moment, is in God Himself; that otherness or Other-Being, the finite, the negative, is not outside of God, and that in its character as otherness it does not hinder unity with God; otherness, the negation, is consciously known to be a moment of the Divine nature.[23]

Here the Son of God is explicitly interpreted as the finite otherness of God the Father. Such texts, among many others, have led James Yerkes to conclude in his outstanding recent study that Hegel "presupposes a doctrine of the Incarnation which is universally ontological in character. That is to say, God becomes *man*— generically, universally, essentially. The *locus* of the Incarnation is mankind and is not just restricted—ontologically speaking—to *one* man."[24] Historically, we know that the left-wing interpretation culminated in a pantheistic humanism that, from a religious point of view, has done much to discredit the whole effort to unify historical and divine Being.

The error of left-wing Hegelianism can be avoided by recalling that, in Christian theology, the meaning of incarnation and creation are of a piece. This suggests an alternative construction of the material content of Christian theology consistent with the historicity of God, an alternative quite close to the thought of John Scotus Erigena.[25] It is the world, and most centrally human life, which is the otherness of God, and the divine self-making is established through the creation of nature and, most importantly, human beings. The Christian belief in the incarnation of God in Jesus should be understood as God continuing to make the world by redeeming it, God continuing to make human life. The history of God is the narrative of divine self-making through continuous world-making. Such a unification of Christian theology and the ontology of historical being avoids the consequences of the left-wing reading of Hegel's philosophical history of Spirit.

These last reflections have been a case study in Christian theology on how to carry out the unification of the material content of Christian belief with the ontology of historical being. The study illustrates some of the insights for Christian theology that follow from thinking of God as historical. Certainly for incarnational religions and theologies, there are ample reasons for taking seriously a conception of the historicity of God. Moreover, for any effort to understand the relation of a divine Being with the human world, tension is mitigated by the notion of divine historicity.

In conclusion, let us return to the philosophical level to ask about the appropriateness of "person" as a cognitive symbol for understanding the Divine. If we are to continue to employ this traditional symbol to bring to focus a philosophical conception of God, it seems to me we should have in mind above all the ontology of historical being. God is superhistorical being and not-being. He is subject who is never object as another being in the world; he is a living presence with an infinite past that is preserved and surpassing future that is anticipated; and as with any living presence, we are able to speak his name and invoke his presence but we are unable to give a fully determinate description, for *theos* was, is, and will be the mighty acts signified by the verbs of world-making.[26]

NOTES

1 Soren Kierkegaard, *Philosophical Fragments,* trans. David Swenson (Princeton: Princeton University Press, 1936), 94.

2 Georg W. F. Hegel, *The Philosophy of History,* trans. J. Sibree (New York: Dover, 1956), 328.

3 The statement is Maurice Merleau-Ponty's in the chapter entitled "Temporality," in *Phenomenology of Perception,* trans. Colin Smith (London: Routledge & Kegan Paul, 1962), 421.

4 Merleau-Ponty's phenomenology confirms this judgment: "If we separate the objective world from the finite perspectives which open upon it, and posit it in itself, we find everywhere in it only so many instances of 'now'" (*Phenomenology of Perception,* 412).

5 For a more detailed discussion of this issue, cf. Raymond Aron, *Introduction to the Philosophy of History,* trans. George J. Irwin (Boston: Beacon, 1961), 22-39, as well as my own "Historicity, Narratives, and the Understanding of Human Life," *The Journal of the British Society for Phenomenology,* forthcoming.

6 This theory of narrative description is most importantly influenced by two authors, Arthur C. Danto, *Analytical Philosophy of History* (Cambridge: Cambridge University Press, 1968); and Frederick A. Olafson, *The Dialectic of Action: A Philosophical Interpretation of History and the Humanities* (Chicago: University of Chicago Press, 1979).

7 Walter Kaufman, "The Hegel Myth and Its Method," in *Hegel: A Collection of Critical Essays,* ed. Alasdair MacIntyre (Garden City, N.Y.: Doubleday, 1972), 21.

8 Cf., e.g., W. B. Gallie, *Philosophy and the Historical Understanding* (New York: Schocken, 1964), chaps. 2-4; as well as the otherwise outstanding essay by Paul Ricoeur, "The Narrative Function," in *Hermeneutics and the Human Sciences,* ed. and trans. John B. Thompson (Cambridge: Cambridge University Press, 1981), 274-96.

9 *The Basic Works of Aristotle,* ed. Richard McKeon (New York: Random House, 1941), *De Poetica,* trans. Ingram Bywater, 1462, 1450b21-27.

10 Georg W. F. Hegel, *The Phenomenology of Spirit,* trans. A. V. Miller (Oxford: Oxford University Press, 1979). The aid of Martin Heidegger's master work, *Being and Time,* trans. John Macquarrie and Edward Robinson (New York: Harper & Row, 1962), is also unmistakeable.

11 Emil Fackenheim, *Metaphysics and Historicity,* The Aquinas Lecture, 1961 (Milwaukee, Wisc.: Marquette University Press, 1961), 28-29. Fackenheim's essay has been a profound help in formulating the ontology of historical being schematized in this essay.

12 Rudolf Bultmann has an excellent account of the development of historical

consciousness in his *History and Eschatology: The Presence of Eternity* (St. Louis, Mo.: Green, 1957). A more detailed, if somewhat more controversial, account may be found in R. G. Collingwood, *The Idea of History* (London: Oxford University Press, 1956), pts. 1-4.

13 It is ultimately Paul Tillich's "method of correlation" that is, in such a statement, being recommended but modified. Cf. Paul Tillich, *Systematic Theology* (Chicago: University of Chicago Press, 1951), 1:60-65.

14 Karl Barth, *The Doctrine of Reconciliation*, vol. 4 of *Church Dogmatics*, trans. Rev. G. W. Bromiley (Edinburgh: T. & T. Clark, 1956), 112.

15 John Scotus Erigena, *On the Division of Nature*, trans. A. B. Wolter, in *Medieval Philosophy: From St. Augustine to Nicholas of Cusa*, ed. John F. Wippel and Allan B. Wolter (New York: The Free Press, 1969), 123.

16 Charles Hartshorne, *A Natural Theology for Our Time* (LaSalle, Ill.: Open Court, 1967), 127. For additional argument supporting the compatibility of historicity with a philosophy of universalities, cf. my "Husserl and History," *The Journal of the British Society for Phenomenology* 11 (1980): 77-91; as well as David Carr, *Phenomenology and the Problem of History* (Evanston, Ill.: Northwestern University Press, 1974), chap. 10.

17 Cf. Erigena, 127-31.

18 Fackenheim offers a brief sketch of the history of the meontological (*me on*:not-being) tradition with respect to God in *Metaphysics and Historicity*, 30-31 n. 20. The appropriateness of meontological thought for philosophical theology is more apparent now that we have a meontological philosophy of person available in Sartre and Heidegger, for both of whom the person or *Dasein* is that being which is a lack of being, whose being presents itself in the form of a question. For a meontology of person that is open to a meontology of God, cf. Emmanuel Levinas, *Totality and Infinity: An Essay on Exteriority*, trans. Alphonso Lingis (Pittsburgh: Duquesne University Press, 1969).

19 Hegel, *Phenomenology of Spirit*, 66. Also cf. Hartshorne, 128; as well as Erigena, 127-31.

20 Hegel, *The Philosophy of History*, 328. I have been able to discover two other explicit uses of the phrase "history of God" in Hegel, both in Hegel's *Lectures on the History of Philosophy*, trans. E. S. Haldane and E. S. Simpson (New York: Humanities Press, 1963), 3:16. I have not found the phrase in the *Phenomenology of Spirit*, although the concept certainly does play largely.

Moreover, in the lectures on *The Philosophy of History*, Hegel describes the whole Old and New Testaments as "narratives" (p. 418).

21 Ibid., 325.

22 Hegel, *Phenomenology of Spirit*, 131.

23 Georg W. F. Hegel, *Lectures on the Philosophy of Religion*, trans. from the 2d German ed. by Rev. E. B. Speirs (London: Kegan Paul, Trench, Trubner, and Co., 1895), 3:98.

24 James Yerkes, *The Christology of Hegel* (Missoula, Mont.: Scholars Press for the American Academy of Religion, 1978), 171-72.

25 Cf. Erigena, 135-37.

26 This paper should not end without tribute to the thought of my teacher, Peter A. Bertocci, whose *The Person God Is* (New York: Humanities, 1970) includes a temporalistic theory of the Divine person. I have refrained from explicit endorsement of the personalist philosophy of religion for two reasons: Prof. Bertocci does not distinguish a temporalistic theory of person from a philosophy of historical existence, a distinction I regard as crucial (I am unable to locate the phrase "history of God" in Prof. Bertocci's writings); and, I do not find it necessarily the case, as does Bertocci, that an ontology of divine historicity indicates that a finitistic theology is called for.

I have also been keenly mindful, throughout these reflections, of the criticisms of any effort to symbolize God as person by another of my teachers, J. N. Findlay, whose theological perspective is summarized in "The Impersonality of God," in *God: The Contemporary Discussion,* ed. Frederick Sontag and M. Darrol Bryant (Barrytown, N.Y.: Unification Theological Seminary, 1982), 181-96.

I am also grateful for the comments and criticisms of Professor Haralds T. Biezais, who was my commentator when I presented an earlier version of this paper at the conference of New ERA in Ft. Lauderdale, Florida, January, 1983. I am also grateful to Professors Peter Bertocci (Boston University) and Arthur Holmes (Wheaton College Illinois) for reading and commenting on the earlier version of this paper.

Does Divine Love Entail Suffering In God?

William J. Hill

U ntil the time of Ludwig Feuerbach theological disputes within Christianity focused on such truths as: the nature of justification, the concept of Church, the divinity of Christ, etc. The one Archimedian point never seriously called into question was that concerning God himself. Whether his existence could be demonstrated, and what arguments might succeed in doing so, had been all along matter for discussion, but not the question of God's reality. Beginning with the late eighteenth century, however, even that ultimate certitude was opened to question. By the mid-nineteenth century the question had become one not only of the truth of God's existing, but of the meaning of all language about the Transcendent to begin with. Is it possible to give any meaning at all to speech about that which by definition lies beyond empirical experience? Wittgenstein's theory of language games marked a first phase of resolution: speech about the Absolute or Transcendent was endowed with meaning on the basis of usage; it meant what its users intended it to mean within the parameters of the language game in which they were engaged. The question of truth, of granting reality to what was the trans-empirical referent of such talk, was simply beyond the reach of all rational discourse. The meaning acknowledged here was not able to be established publically, but was mutually agreed upon on noncognitive grounds by those of a given religious commitment.

But if theology is to function, if there is to be any talk about God whatsoever in an attempt at objectivity, then some notion of God has to be presupposed. This leaves theists in the dilemma of having to choose, seemingly, between language that is anthropomorphic on one hand and agnostic on the other. In the first option, the "infinite qualitative difference" (Kierkegaard) is slighted and God is treated as one more entity of the world, even if the most perfect of all. In the second option, it is acknowledged that human speech does not reach the divine at all, and words applied to God are empty of all meaning.

Curiously enough, recent attempts to surmount this dichotomy, between anthropomorphism on one hand and agnosticism on the other tend to foster a nuanced version of the first alternative, namely anthropomorphism. This is true in theologies which view religious language as paradoxical (Barth), mythological (Bultmann), symbolic (Tillich), or analogical—either in the sense of Process theology which tends to treat analogy as univocal speech, or in the sense of existential theology which is open to analogy on the level of *Existenz*. Religious language in the Christian tradition, largely sacral in tone, has lost its hold on believers who live in an all-pervasive secular world. This secularism, coupled with the atheist critique of the past century, has made it difficult for men and women of contemporary experience to believe in a gracious and efficacious God. Present-day Christian theology, then, is witnessing a massive effort at recovering relevance. The overwhelming tendency is to trim the transcendence once ascribed to God on the grounds that such a God remains remote from and unconcerned with affairs that are human-sized. The thesis of this paper will be that it is precisely God's utter transcendence of and autonomy from the world that explains his universal and intimate involvement with every finite reality and event; the ground of God's immanence then is precisely his transcendence.

Rudolf Bultmann's God reveals not the holy mystery which he himself is, but the depths of human self-understanding. Herbert Braun carries the demythological project further, seeing the concept of God which underlies the language of the New Testament as merely a cultural inheritance from Judaism. Such language is used purely as a means for conveying a message which overthrows the original meaning of the literature, namely, one affirming an omnipotent creator God. Scriptural references to God as transcendent are not to be taken literally, then. Jürgen Moltmann—and less radically, Wolfhart Pannenberg—advance a notion of deity that replaces eternity conceived as timelessness with a form of primal temporality that has the effect of historicizing God. Process theologians, taking their cue from Alfred North Whitehead, balance off infinity as only one pole of God's nature, with finitude as characteristic of the other pole—adding that only the latter, the finite—accounts for actuality in God. Charles Hartshorne is thus characteristic of Process thinkers in developing a concept that gives preeminence to the relativity of God, who needs the world as much as the world needs him. The immutable and so timeless God of classical theism is understood as incapable of entering into a relationship with an everchanging and temporal world. The assumption is that if God stands outside any temporal series, there seems no way of explaining how that series can matter to him at all. Adrian Thatcher carries the complaint further, asking "How is God personal who cannot experience sorrow, sadness, and pain, i.e., experiences which help constitute us as persons and contribute to our personal growth when we encounter them?"[1]

What is happening in all this is a move away from classical theism in the direction of what is generally understood as panentheism, defined as a doctrine which constitutes divinity as neither identical with the world (pantheism) nor as autonomous from it (classical theism), but as in a state of dependence upon it. What comes to the fore in this kind of thinking is the category of Becoming, not as excluding the category of Being but as entering into a dialectical and polar relationship with Being, in constituting the divine reality. Nonetheless, a certain ontological priority is ceded to Becoming over Being—with two important consequences for contemporary Christian theology. One is an emphasis upon the future over past and present, so that even God's being is grasped in terms of futurity; he is "the power of the future" (Pannenberg) or "the promise of the future" (Moltmann).[2] The other is a turn to the subject in its activity as self-enacting and self-positing, so that God is conceived of as the Absolute Subject.

The most graphic consequence of this theological orientation, however, is felt in the endeavor to explain what is meant by designating God as a God of love. All Christian denominations, from radical neo-orthodoxy to extreme neo-liberalism, share in the consensus that no other concept epitomizes more richly and more ultimately the deity of God. Nor is such understanding limited to Christian thought. For the Christian, it is the mere appropriation of the simple "God is love" of the First Letter of John (4:16), but it has clear grounding in the piety of the Jewish scriptures. It is entirely lacking, moreover, in both Plato and Aristotle. This is clearly the case in Aristotle for whom any love of the finite and the limited by the First Unmoved Mover would only detract from the latter's absorption with its own infinite being and goodness. For Plato, if the occasional beneficence of the gods might justly be called a love for mankind, this is only a side effect of divine self love, the *eros* on the part of the gods seeking their own fulfillment in striving to share in the subsistent form of goodness. Both Plotinus and Spinoza encourage us to love God, but caution against being misled into thinking of God as personal—an implicit denial that God himself is capable of any love save a form of self-love.

But this central Christian affirmation—that God is love—faces one well-nigh insurmountable obstacle: the objection lodged by the undeniable existence of evil and suffering in the world. Indeed, in our present state of heightened consciousness and concern, it is not simply the fact of human suffering but an overwhelming abundance and proliferation of it on all sides that challenges taking seriously the conviction that God is nowise a God of evil but entirely a God of love. The dilemma here is well-known and needn't be rehearsed in detail. Either God is powerless against the forces of evil in the world, capable at the most of merely mitigating somewhat its destructive power, and then is not omnipotent and so suffers a diminution of his deity, or he does possess such power but chooses not to exercise it to any significant degree, in which case he no longer qualifies as a God of love.

The resolutions offered historically to this dilemma are multiple and varied, but no one of them can lay claim to being an adequate answer; all of them leave important questions unanswered. In itself evil rises before us as a surd, intractable to rational analysis. Thus, ultimately evil poses itself, not as a problem which can be solved or circumvented, but as a mystery hidden in the designs of God with which we must continue to live.

Thus, believers continue to believe in an all-loving God in spite of the unexplained phenomenon of innocent suffering in the world. They refuse to allow the arational spectre of evil to count against faith in God. For this reason, atheists and humanists consider belief in God to be without rational grounding.

Organized religions have tended traditionally to share the view that God himself is not the direct cause of evil in creation, but even this position has been challenged—in psychology by Carl Jung,[3] in philosophy by Frederick Sontag. The latter dismisses the all-good God developed in Christian Platonism and writes, "The flaws that lead to man's downfall must find their source in God's nature or else go unexplained."[4] C. E. Rolt does, however, develop the extraordinary position in which evil comes from God in the sense that he refuses to create it. That creative act establishes order out of chaos, and God's exclusion of evil from what he does create leaves that chaos with a positive and ever threatening power vis-à-vis good creation.[5] Cognate to this but less radical is a solution, based on a metaphysical presupposition running through dialectical thinking from Hegel to Tillich, that God is Being-Itself *(Sein-Selbst)* constantly asserting itself over and against the negativizing influence of nonbeing. Thus, Tillich can write, "It is the nature of blessedness itself that requires a negative element in the eternity of Divine Life."[6] This avoids introducing evil into the interior of God, as something intrinsic to his deity—thus, it absolves God from blame for evil in the world. But it achieves this by locating evil as a surd entirely alien to God, contrary to his will but outside his control. Creation itself is then an attempt on God's part to hold back the power of darkness, a dynamic striving to overcome them. Process theology is sympathetic towards this outlook to which, however, it gives expression in a totally different conceptual scheme. Here God's dependence upon the world in his consequent nature does not make him the source of evil, but it does render him susceptible to the suffering which the world cannot avoid due to its own radical finitude. Though God transforms all values he derives from the world and rejects all disvalues, still his advance into the future cannot ever be other than finite at any given point. The consequence of this is that though God resists all evil, he does experience in his physical feelings or prehensions, human suffering (which in an indirect way can frequently turn out to be something beneficial). In this way, compassion becomes an attribute of God, so that Whitehead himself can describe God as "a fellow-sufferer who understands."[7]

The *Pathos* of God

The most original and challenging way of dealing theologically with this question of how the loving will of God can be reconciled with the phenomenon of a human world wounded deeply by anguish and suffering is one offered in the provocative thinking of Jürgen Moltmann.[8] His initial presupposition is that we have no grounds for assuming that *in himself* (as what Luther calls the *Deus Absconditus*) God is other than all-good and all-powerful, so that he is neither the source of evil in the world nor is his beingness affected untowardly or diminished by the pain of the world. All such negativity arises, then, from this world, due either to its ontological finitude (this is the risk involved in creation as God "lets be" the world) or (as Moltmann seemingly prefers) due to the negativity of human history culminating in its rejection of God. However, in an act of altruistic love, grounded in his uncreated freedom, God, who apart from such a choice is not a God for mankind, chooses freely to become a God of and for men in a relationship of unconditional love (Luther's *Deus Revelatus*). The voice of Karl Barth can clearly be heard here as an undertone to Moltmann's own, and his (Moltmann's) commitment to Evangelical and Reformed theology becomes manifest, in such themes as revelation, human iniquity, and election—the last of these, however, is given a universality it did not originally possess.

Be that as it may, love by definition is a unitive force in which the lover unites himself with the beloved in the most real and most intimate of ways, entering into and taking upon himself everything that qualifies the existence of the beloved, whether bettering or worsening that existing. But the beloved in this case exists only in an environment of evil and the all-pervasive suffering that accompanies it. It is here that Moltmann's contribution appears in all the power of its originality. God does not simply act in the world so as to bring to an end the reign of the powers of darkness, offering forgiveness to men and women, and eliminating all suffering. This is reasonably said in light of the undeniable perdurance of both evil and human anguish, perhaps even their intensification today.

Without denying that God could have acted in this way, at least diminishing radically the proliferation of negative factors, Moltmann envisages the divine love as inaugurating salvation in a quite different and more profound way. God in effect assumes human suffering into his own being, making it to be his suffering. It is possible to conceive of a world from which all suffering has been precluded simply by God's willing to vanquish and banish from it all evil. But the price of this would be a curtailment of human freedom. At least the love for God as a totally autonomous act springing from finite freedoms would necessarily be compromised. Building on an observation of Albert Camus, Moltmann makes the suggestive remark that man can gain ascendency over God in one act—that of freely embracing his own death.[9] If tradition has long assumed that such an action is impossible to God, Moltmann wishes to suggest that such is not the case at all.

Moltmann's contention is, in effect, that love constitutes the very essence of God, and that by definition demands the "other" as its object. This cannot be supplied for by presupposing the Christian doctrine of the Trinity in total autonomy from creation because the members of that tri-unity are not other than God. Thus, God requires a world consummated with the creature that, in freedom, is capable both of receiving divine love and responding to it. This is the motivation both of God's act of creating and of his becoming incarnate as man. But this "requirement" is not anything demanded by God's nature; it is elicited in total freedom by his love.

> God does not suffer out of deficiency of being, like created beings. To that extent he is "apathetic." But he suffers from the love which is the superabundance and overflowing of his being. In so far he is "pathetic".[10]

At this point, it would seem that Moltmann's thought, by its own inner logic demands something like Luther's distinction between the *Deus Absconditus* and *Deus Revelatus*. Because we cannot know the "hidden God" he must be left free of all engagement in human affairs; it is the "revealed God" who is known to us, and known as involved fully with human misery. This distinction safeguards the gratuity of God's decision to take within himself the suffering of mankind. Eberhard Jüngel approximates this theological view when, after insisting that "God's being is in becoming," he adds that one must not confuse this "with other statements such as, God's being is becoming, or, God's being becomes in becoming."[11] Nonetheless, both Jüngel and Moltmann minimize the implications of this distinction: Jüngel in his claim that there is "no being of God in-and-for-itself without man";[12] Moltmann with the statements "He has to be man and nothing but man" and "the cross of Christ is not something that is historically fortuitous, which might not have happened."[13] What prompts this reservation on the Lutheran distinction is the desire to historicize God's being. Thus an even more explicit assertion of Moltmann's suggests giving up "the distinction made in the early church and in tradition between the 'God in himself' and the 'God for us'..." with the consequence that "the nature of God would have to be the human history of Christ and not a divine 'nature' separate from man."[14]

Still and all, God cannot assume a state of suffering except historically; this is possible only if God is there with men and so as a man. Yet the Incarnation is not a contingency plan for redeeming fallen mankind; rather it is willed for the sake of achieving a full love relationship.[15] A possible misunderstanding must be avoided here. It is not a question of God willing suffering to men as punishment for sin, and then taking that punishment upon himself. The Japanese theologian Kazoh Kitamori has put this graphically in noting that God is displeased with our sins but does not suffer because of them; what causes his suffering is his own conflict in choosing to love us even as we remain under his wrath.[16] The point is, however, that the nature of love is such that its full realization is achieved only in passing through suffering. In order to be completely itself, love must suffer, so true is this that "one who cannot suffer cannot love." Similarly, God "has to go through time... for ...it is only in this way that he is eternal."[18] And it is a question of suffering in his very divinity; there is no question here of limiting such suffering to only the humanity which God has assumed. "Suffering is in God's being itself."[19] Moltmann advocates nothing less than a genuine panentheism.

In this process, God identifies himself with mankind so as to stand over against (as it were) his own deity. For this to be intelligible means that God must undergo within himself a process of self-differentiation.[20] For Judaism, this is the differentiation that Yahweh effects between himself and his dwelling in the midst of his chosen people, the Shekinah Yahweh. For Christianity, this duality becomes a trinity. What are called the trinitarian processions are nothing less than divine history. Somewhat differently stated—the history of the world is taken up into God as his trinitarian history.[21] It means that God undergoes a sundering within himself wherein the Son of God is delivered over to the forces of evil, occasioning suffering (differing somewhat in mode) on the part of both the Father and the Son. Since this rendering within God is motivated by love, it overthrows evil which ultimately is explained as the refusal to love. Thus God's suffering is the transformation of evil into good. This originates the second phase of God's history, one in which the Spirit of that love, in its unitive power, rejoins the Son to the Father. In this, the Son bears with him all of suffering mankind who have become reconciled with the Father through him.

Some General Reservations

Several reservations of a general sort on Moltmann's original and challenging thought here assert themselves rather quickly. One is the not so covert Hegelianism—especially evident in the early Moltmann's choice of the Marxist thinker, Ernst Bloch, as his dialogue partner. The implication of this Hegelian background is that God's freedom is somewhat constrained by a controlling idea of historical process as subject to the dialectic of thought—of affirmation, negation, and then synthesis or sublation *(Aufhebung)*. Another is the historicizing of God's being, which has the effect of collapsing the immanent Trinity into the economic Trinity. Thirdly, cognate to these is the emphasis upon futurity as the mode of divine being, which has the effect of emptying out the past and especially the present of any lasting meaningfulness. What will follow here, however, is a specific reflection, critical in kind, on Moltmann's contention that love in God entails by necessity suffering in God.

Divine Love as More than *Pathos*

Moltmann's support for his thesis is that love demands a surrender to the "other" in virtue of which the lover is rendered open and vulnerable. This giving of the self means a vulnerability to possible rejection by the beloved, but also to whatever negative factors may be afflicting the beloved. The unitive power of love is such that whatever evils befall the beloved, also work their negative effect upon the lover; in this sense the beloved is "another self." This is surely true of love as a passion, that is as a psychosomatic phenomenon rooted in bodiliness. But very few religions predicate bodiliness of God. It also can be true of love as volitional, as a free disposition of spirit, but this need not be the case. Genuine compassion, meaning voluntarily sharing the suffering of one's friend in an attempt to alleviate his or her pain, characterizes love as finite, not love as such. The core reality of love as such is the affective union with another or others. The primary manifestation of this is a willing of good to that person, not for one's own sake (unless one is involved only in a love of desire *amor concupiscentiae*, which is love in an utilitarian sense), but for the other's own sake (which is a true love of benevolence, *amor benevolentiae*). If the beloved is in a state of anguish, then the impulse of love is directed towards alleviating that anguish to the extent of its powers. Only when its resources are exhausted due to its finitude, is it content with compassion for the friend in a loving endeavor to lessen this misery by sharing it in a vicarious and sympathetic way. Compassion, then (as opposed to mere pity) characterizes love, not as such but in its finite modes.

But divine love is omnipotent, capable of overcoming whatever evil befalls mankind. This means that God enlists himself on man's side, and in support of the human cause, ranging himself against all forms of evil and suffering. For such love to be operative, however, does not demand that God be a co-sufferer in his divine nature. Tillich's reservation here is well taken when he writes that such a view "brings God down to the level of the passionate and suffering gods of Greek mythology."[22] It is this uniqueness of divine being, whereby God does not and cannot suffer in himself, that explains why he can love unfathomably, in a totally altruistic way, why divine love can be what the New Testament calls *agape* rather than only the self-fulfilling *eros* of Greek rational thought.

For God to love another is to will good creatively and efficaciously to that other, insofar as God is a creator and redeemer transcending all finite reality. This is not a mere sympathetic and compassionate but ultimately impotent love; it is more than the divine *pathos* of which Moltmann speaks. To maintain this is to acknowledge the immutability of God in the sense that, as the

64

creative source and ground of all that is, God is already the fullness of being. Any change in his being means either the acquisition of something previously lacking, or the loss of some perfection previously possessed. But this is to say no more than that God is not susceptible to change *in the way that creatures are.* Immutability remains a negative concept, denying to God all forms of creaturely alteration; though it does intend to designate a positive divine attribute, this is something that we can neither know nor represent in itself. Moltmann's view that God suffers in himself is, in effect, to have God will to be something less than God; even the Christian belief that God became man does not gainsay this since the Incarnation does not imply a metamorphosis of divinity into humanity.

The point of all this is that God can love without suffering, even granting the state of mankind as one of misery. If he does in fact choose to suffer, then the reason for this is not any inner logic of the attribute of love itself, but God's utter freedom in willing for mankind a role in its own reconciliation with himself; the reasons lie on man's side rather than God's. So, it is one thing to deny that God can suffer *in his divinity,* and another to acknowledge that he does suffer *in and through* the humanity he has made one with himself. Christian piety and theology have nearly always maintained that the truth cannot be captured in the expression that "the humanity which God has made one with himself suffers"; it has with some consistency maintained that "it is God himself who suffers, though in and through his humanity." This is not to forget that this understanding came to the fore rather gradually, and that many of the pre-Chalcedonian Fathers, especially those of the school of Antioch, resist the suggestion that God himself suffers and dies, and that some even go so far as to deny that the humanity of Christ suffers in any genuine sense of the word, e.g., the monophysites and the followers of Apollinarius. The former position exaggerates the distinction of the two natures in Christ and slights thereby the unity; the latter position assumes the opposite stance and so exaggerates the unity to the point where any admission of suffering on the part of the humanity is tantamount to admitting suffering on the part of the Logos of God. The Arians and Adoptionists believed that the undeniable suffering of the humanity argued against predicating divinity of Christ in any proper sense.

Ultimately, however, it is the bolder language of the New Testament that prevails: it is the "author of life" who is killed (Acts 3:15); it is "the Lord of glory" who is crucified (1 Cor. 2:8); it is he whose "state is divine...who...empties himself...even to accepting death" (Phil. 2:6ff.). Such language is adopted without being trimmed by any philosophical doctrine of God's impassibility, by Irenaeus, Tertullian, Origen, Anthanasius, Hilary, and others. After Chalcedon it becomes unchallenged in orthodox circles.

It is not a question, either, of *saying* that God suffers and dies, but meaning that really it is only the humanity united to him that does so. Rather God himself undergoes such agony—but in his humanity and not in his divinity. Medieval theology explained this in terms of the well-known *communicatio idiomatum,* a theory maintaining that attributes of divinity predicated of the Logos, and attributes of divinity predicated of the man Jesus—due to the unification of the two natures as enhypostatic in the person of the Word. Though this theory concerned itself with matters of speech, it was understood as grounded in the state of affairs prevailing in reality.

If this be true, it follows that the suffering which God truly experiences, and in the profoundest way, does not result in any qualitative change or diminution of God's nature. Thus it seems possible to safeguard divine immutability and impassibility, without denying the incredible truth of revelation that God wills to suffer in and through the suffering of his people.

Process theology prefers to locate both impassibility and passibility within the divine nature itself—the former in the primordial nature, the latter in the consequent nature. But if that distinction of natures is real, it jeopardizes the divine unity and simplicity. If it is a rational distinction on our part (as would seem to be the case) then it only calls attention to the truth that God transcends both our concepts, that of passibility on one hand, and its negation (impassibility) on the other. If so, we need to employ both notions in speaking of God who lies beyond our understanding of ontic immunity from suffering and yet opens himself voluntarily to the ravages of suffering.

The problem, then, is one of how to relate these conflicting concepts of deity in some dialectical fashion. H. P. Owen has attempted to put this truth into words by noting that to deny that

God *changes* is not to deny that he *responds* to evil in the world; indeed, it is because he is changeless that he is capable of responding perfectly.[23] He makes another attempt at this in allowing that "God suffers on account of finite evil [but] his sufferings do not modify his perfection."[24] Other authors have striven to capture the intentionality behind some such distinction as this. In every case what is involved is the awareness that love can be predicated of God only analogically. And analogy only seeks a qualified similarity between entities radically different from one another. Karl Rahner, for example, insists that God changes and suffers, not in himself but in his other—meaning in the humanity of Christ, though it is God himself who changes.[25] The distinction is perhaps an overly subtle one and may appear as merely a verbal solution to the problem. But it does allow God to be involved in human affairs, including the negative ones, without sacrificing the idea of God as Pure Actuality. W. Norris Clarke offers help in denying that God can change in the sense of "moving to a qualitatively higher level of inner perfection" while granting that "God's inner being is genuinely affected, not in an ascending or descending way, but in a truly real, personal, conscious, rational way by his relations with us."[26] Another possibility is to argue from the irreducibility of the distinction between the notions of nature and person or persons in God. This might enable one to say that in his nature God remains ever changeless, while in his personhood he is capable of altering in virtue of the fact that the latter category is understood as a pure relation to other persons, divine and created.[27] The advantage here lies in not viewing God's becoming man as a union of two natures, divine and human (even understanding this as a *hypostatic union,* i.e., a unification in hypostasis or person), but as a unity wherein the person of the Son of God is the ultimate subject of the human nature (perhaps better called a *hypostatic unity*). When finite entities change, God knows and loves them in their changed situation, thus it has to be granted that the divine knowing and loving change at least on the part of their terminative objects. God then knows and loves something new *in the world* and though he gathers this novelty into himself, this need not mean any increment to his own plenitude of being which already pre-contains everything that is or possibly could be. Hans Urs von Balthasar approaches the question in explicit terms of what is really conveyed by the statement that it is God who suffers. Death means a radical severing of all ties with God (thus its ominous character). If one is to speak of the death of God, then, this cannot be reduced to a transaction between God and the man Jesus. Rather there occurs a genuine abandonment of the Son by the Father, so that it is God himself who experiences the God-forsakenness of death.[28] "God did not spare his own Son but gave him up to benefit us all" (Rom. 8:32). Some similar version of this solution is espoused by Eberhard Jüngel, Hans Küng, and Heribert Mühlen, among others within conceptual schemes of their own.[29]

The conclusion, then, is: first, that God remains immutable and impassible in his own intrinsic godhead, so that his genuine love for creatures cannot entail suffering within divinity as such; but secondly, that God does choose to enter personally and relationally into the heart of mankind's suffering in his transcendentally free and loving response to it. God truly suffers, not (as Moltmann would have it) in his very deity, but in and through his humanity which is one with the humanity of all men and women.

This, however, leaves us with one enormous question: Why? One solution that continues to urge itself is some adaptation of that first proposed, somewhat primitively perhaps, by Anselm of Canterbury.[30] At the root of human suffering (as opposed to natural evils such as floods and earthquakes which God wills indirectly for the sake of that gradation in being and dynamic interaction of forces which characterizes the cosmos as a physical whole) lies malice and rebellion, made possible by the freedom to gainsay God, which is the one power over God possessed by man. In the Judeo-Christian tradition, this is conveyed by the symbol of "sin." Suffering which is not sin because it touches the innocent as much as the perpetrators of evil, nonetheless follows a certain connaturality in the wake of sin. Suffering, thus, is not moral evil, but evil of natural defect as such has its negative effect upon man who is able to register it in a conscious way. This disruption of order and tranquility arises from some primordial act or acts of malice, one which is universal in affecting indiscriminately the entire human family. It is totally reconcilable with an evolutionary theory concerning human origins, since it can be conceived of as occurring at some given moment on the evolutionary scale. In response to this, however, God's love takes upon itself freely a modality whereby the powers of darkness are overthrown, not by an act of divine omnipotence, but by God himself becoming the subject *(hypostasis)* of an act of human love which negates dialectically that primordial human act which was the refusal to love, i.e., an act of resistance to God's loving will.

God chooses not to cancel out human malice by himself on the ontic plane (thus malice continues to work negatively in the world today) but rather to inaugurate a divine-human act of love wherein man himself enters into the heart of evil by accepting the suffering which is the residue of moral evil, and overthrowing that evil from within. This is in order that human freedom, responsible for its alienation from God in the first place, of which suffering is a sign (it is not a question of suffering as a punishment for sin) might be involved in its restoration with God. Anselm called this "satisfaction," a term laden with forensic implications, many of them deriving from twelfth-century feudalism. Aquinas, taking this thought over from Anselm, moderates it by transposing it from the order of strict justice on God's part to the domain of divine love and mercy.[31] What Amselm intends, however, is that only man is obliged whereas only God is able—an expression which indicates the redemptive power of all human suffering undergone in response to God's "becoming sin for our sakes" (2 Cor. 5:21). What all of this amounts to is a genuine Christian panentheism, wherein God who lies beyond suffering in his divinity, chooses freely to suffer as man for mankind.

NOTES

1 Adrian Thatcher, "Concepts of Deity: A Criticism of H. P. Owen," *Anglican Theological Review* 58, no. 3 (July 1976): 300.

2 Cf. Wolfhart Pannenberg, *The Idea of God and Human Freedom*, trans. R. A. Wilson (Philadelphia: Westminster Press, 1971), 111; Jürgen Moltmann, *Theology of Hope*, trans. J. W. Leitch (New York: Harper & Row, 1967), 143f.

3 Cf. Carl Jung, *Psychology and Religion: West and East*, vol. 11 of *Answer to Job* (Princeton, N.J.: Princeton University Press, 1969); here Jung's conviction that all life could be grasped only in polar symbols led him to posit a principle of evil within divinity.

4 Frederick Sontag, *The God of Evil: An Argument from the Existence of the Devil* (New York: Harper & Row, 1970), 130.

5 C. E. Rolt, *The World's Redemption* (London, 1913), 95; cited by Jürgen Moltmann, *The Trinity and the Kingdom*, trans. M. Kohl (San Francisco: Harper & Row, 1981), 34.

6 Paul Tillich, *Systematic Theology* (Chicago: University of Chicago Press, 1963), 3:405.

7 Alfred North Whitehead, *Process and Reality* (New York: Free Press, 1969), 413 (p. 532 in original Macmillan ed. of 1929).

8 Jürgen Moltmann, *The Crucified God*, trans. R. A. Wilson and J. Bowdwin (New York: Harper & Row, 1973), and *The Trinity and the Kingdom*.

9 Moltmann, *The Crucified God*, 222.

10 Moltmann, *The Trinity and the Kingdom*, 23.

11 Eberhard Jüngel, *The Doctrine of the Trinity: God's Being is in Becoming* (Grand Rapids, Mich.: Eerdmans, 1976), 102 n. 155.

12 Jüngel, 108 n. 160.

13 Moltmann, *The Trinity and the Kingdom*, 32-33.

14 Moltmann, *The Crucified God*, 239.

15 Moltmann, *The Trinity and the Kingdom*, 46; his exact words are "The incarnation of God's Son is not an answer to sin. It is the fulfillment of God's eternal longing to become man and to make of every man a god out of grace."

16 Kazoh Kitamori, *Theology of the Pain of God*, trans. M. E. Bratcher (Richmond, Va.: John Knox, 1965), 115.

17 Moltmann, *The Crucified God*, 222.

18 Moltmann, *The Trinity and the Kingdom*, 34, citing C. E. Rolt.

19 Moltmann, *The Crucified God*, 227.

20 Moltmann, *The Trinity and the Kingdom*, 30.

21 Moltmann, *The Crucified God*, 246.

22 Tillich, 404.

23 H. P. Owen, *Concepts of Deity* (New York: Herder and Herder, 1971), 145.

24 Ibid., 88.

25 Karl Rahner, "On the Theology of the Incarnation," *Theological Investigations* 4: esp. 113 n. 3.

26 W. Norris Clarke, *The Philosophical Approach to God*, ed. W. E. Ray (Winston-Salem, N.C.: Wake Forest University, 1979), 104.

27 Cf. W. J. Hill, "Does the World Make a Difference to God?," *The Thomist* 38, no. 1 (January 1974): 146-64.

28 Hans Urs von Balthasar, "Le Mystère Pascal," *Mysterium Salutis*, tome 3, vol. 12 (Paris: Éditions du Cerf, 1972), 13-264.

29 Jüngel; Hans Küng, *Incarnation de Dieu: Introduction á la pensèe thèologique de Hegel comme prolègoménes a une christologie future*, trans. E. Galichet and C. Haas-Smets of *Menschwerdung Gottes* (Paris: Desclèe de Brouwer, 1973), esp. Excursus II, 640-49; Heribert Mühlen, *Die Veränderlichkeit Gottes als Horisont einer zukunftigen Christologie. Auf dem Wege zu einer Kreuzestheologie in Auseinadersetzung mit der altkirchlichen Christologie*, 2d ed. (Munster, 1976).

30 Anselm of Canterbury, *Cur Deus Homo?*, ed. F. S. Schmitt (Munich: International Publications Service, 1956).

31 Thomas Aquinas, *Summa Theologiae*, III, q. 48, a. 2.

Over-Power and God's Responsibility for Sin

Nelson C. Pike

I shall assume that if God exists and is omnipotent, then with respect to any possible event (E) God has power sufficient to determine whether or not E occurs. This is to say that if God exists and is omnipotent, he has control with respect to the occurrence or nonoccurrence of every possible event. And because it would be hard to find a theologian of consequence in the Western tradition who would not accept this thesis, I shall refer to it throughout as the "traditional" doctrine of divine omnipotence. Now allow that the performance of an action on the part of a created agent counts as an event. It follows that if God exists and is omnipotent, he has power sufficient to determine whether or not a given action is performed by a given agent. God has control even with respect to the actions performed by other beings. What, then, of the power of created agents? In an article published in 1978 entitled "Freedom Within Omnipotence," Linwood Urban and Douglas Walton maintain that if omnipotence is understood in the way just suggested, then if there exists an omnipotent being, that being "exhausts all the power in the universe leaving no room for other centers of power." The idea of human freedom to control (even partially) some of the events of the world is, then, what they call an "illusion." The consequence is that created beings cannot be held responsible for anything that happens—not even their own actions. And applying this conclusion to the topic of the problem of evil, Urban and Walton claim: "One can easily see that this result is disastrous for those who hope to solve the problem of evil at least partially by placing the blame for some of the evil in the world upon men."[1] If God alone has power, then he alone is responsible. Given that someone in the world is to be blamed, he is really the only one it could be.

As a general remark, the claim that there is logical conflict between the idea of creaturely freedom and traditional thinking about the nature of God has usually been argued not by reference to the doctrine of divine omnipotence but by reference to the notion of divine omniscience. I here have in mind the problem of divine foreknowledge—an issue widely discussed in antiquity and currently commanding considerable attention among contemporary philosophers. According to Anthony Flew, however, while it is (as he says) "rash" to suggest that divine omniscience (foreknowledge) presents any threat to the idea of human freedom, (in his words) "the problem really begins with omnipotence." Flew continues: "As Creator (God) must be first cause, prime mover, supporter and controller of every thought and action throughout his utterly dependent universe. In short: if creation is in, autonomy is out." This Flew tells us is a "vital conclusion" that is often ignored.[2] Subsequent discussion makes clear that by "autonomy" Flew means creaturely free will[3] and that it, rather than God considered as omnipotent creator, is definitely in. Precisely this same thesis has been urged by advocates of (so-called) Process theology. In the first full length study of the problem of evil from the (so-called) Process point of view, David Griffin (following Hartshorne) claims that if God is omnipotent in the traditional sense, then God has "all the power" and this, he says, is quite incompatible with a manifest metaphysical truth, viz., that there are beings other than God with power to (partially) determine their own activities and the activities of other beings.[4] Thus, while the view we are here considering has not enjoyed much in the way of historical visability, it is among the challenges currently confronting traditional Christian theism. And of course, if God's omnipotence really is incompatible with creaturely freedom, then Urban and Walton are right in extending the conclusion to a negative judgment on one of the more important theological responses to the problem of evil, i.e., the view that creatures, rather than God, are responsible for at least the portion of the evil in the world that consists in and results from their own, freely chosen, immoral actions. Though it would have other unfortunate consequences for Christian theology as well, given the abundance of recent literature on the topic of free will and evil, this one would be of very special interest to contemporary philosophers of religion.

In this paper I am going to argue two nested points. First, the doctrine of omnipotence formulated above carries no negative implications as regards the existence of creaturely freedom. Urban and Walton as well as other philosophers and theologians who have argued to the contrary are wrong about this. But, secondly, if God is omnipotent in the sense specified above, then any theodicy in which it is held that God is not responsible for the performance of immoral actions on the part of the created agents is false. I should add that I regard the second of these points as the central thesis of this paper. The first is argued partly to dispel the misunderstandings of those who have denied it but mostly because the resulting clarification of the notion of divine omnipotence establishes a context in which the second point can be made clear.

Postscript: Throughout, I assume that an omnipotent being is one who has power sufficient to determine the occurrence or nonoccurrence of any possible event. I specify the notion of omnipotence in this way rather than in terms of God's ability to bring about possible states of affairs because in this paper I am interested in omnipotence as it relates to *actions;* and I take actions to be events (occurrences, happenings) rather than states of affairs. Further, I realize that the formula I am using to express the notion of omnipotence is subject to a variety of counterexamples. For instance, there are some things that might be thought of as possible events that no being (however powerful) could determine because they are not determinable, e.g., two plus two equaling four. Then, too, the undetermined event E and the undetermined-by-an-omnipotent-being event E could not be determined by an omnipotent being. Of particular interest in the present discussion are events involving the free agency of finite beings, for instance, Jones freely raising his arm or Jones freely choosing to raise his arm. I assume that any such event could be determined only by the relevant finite being and thus, like the above, could not be determined by an omnipotent God. I suspect that most counterexamples of this sort could be accommodated were I to specify God's omnipotence as "power sufficient to determine any possible event E where 'God determines E' is consistent." But since the argument of this paper neither depends upon nor (so far as I can see) trespasses against refinements that would be needed to transform the formula I am using into a fully adequate analysis, I shall not invite distraction by trying to work them out and then fumbling to carry them along in the present discussion.

Over-Power

I shall begin by developing the concept that will play the leading role in my discussion—the concept of over-power. Here I shall proceed *via* a series of reflections on four diagrams representing four electrical circuits. This first section might best be thought of as an exercise in *a priori* electrical engineering—a study of the concept of control in plain and humble physical dress. I hasten to add that this procedure is taken directly from Urban and Walton. The following pieces of technical apparatus are at least inspired by them as well.

Let us agree that an agent has *positive control* with respect to a given event (E) if that agent has power so to act as to make a causal contribution to the occurrence of E. Correlatively, an agent has *negative control* with respect to E if that agent has power so to act as to make a causal contribution to the nonoccurrence of E, i.e., the occurrence of not-E. There are two subcases under each of these. An agent has *full* positive control with respect to E if that agent has power *sufficient* to effect or secure E. An agent has *partial* positive control with respect to E if that agent has power so to act as to supply a *necessary* (though not a sufficient) condition for the occurrence of E. So also for negative control. An agent's negative control is full if that agent has power sufficient to secure not-E. It is partial if it is within that agent's power so to act as to supply a necessary (though not a sufficient) condition for not-E. As a final piece of operating equipment, let us say that an agent has *complete control* with respect to E if that agent has full positive control and full negative control with respect to E.

Now, as a warm up, consider the following two electric circuits with two agents (Arthur and Bailey) stationed at the switches

76

A and B respectively. Allow that Arthur and Bailey are independent agents, i.e., neither can effect the actions of the other. Let E be the bulb pictured at the top of the diagram coming on. Not-E is the bulb going off:

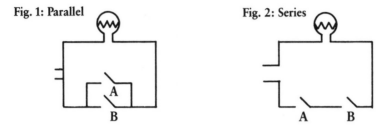

Fig. 1: Parallel

Fig. 2: Series

In the situation diagrammed in Fig. 1 (the parallel circuit), both Arthur and Bailey have full positive control with respect to E. This is because Arthur can effect E by closing A and Bailey can effect E by closing B. However, neither has full negative control. Not-E results only if both switches are open. Thus, in this circumstance, both Arthur's and Bailey's negative control is only partial. Thus, neither has complete control with respect to E. In the situation portrayed in Fig. 2 (the series circuit), we get the same final result but in reverse manner. Here Arthur and Bailey both have full negative control but neither has full positive control. This is because each can secure not-E by opening his own switch, but neither can effect E by himself. To effect E, both Arthur and Bailey must close their respective switches. Thus, in this case, Arthur's positive control and Bailey's positive control are both partial. Hence, again, neither Arthur nor Bailey have complete control with respect to E.

Could we consider a circuit having switches operated by two independent agents and in which one of those agents has complete control with respect to E? By itself, this would not be difficult:

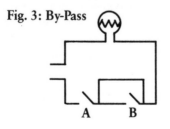

Fig. 3: By-Pass

Here, Arthur has complete control. He can effect E by closing A and he can secure not-E by opening A. And how about Bailey? He can work his switch, but he is not in position to make a causal contribution to the occurrence or nonoccurrence of E. He has been by-passed and thus has no control—full or partial. It is as if we had a circuit with only one switch (A) and Arthur alone to determine whether the light goes on or off.

This, then, provokes the next question—one that may be more difficult to answer than the last—*viz.*, could we construct a circuit in which one agent has complete control and in which a second agent has at least some (partial) control with respect to E? This question is of special interest in the present discussion since we are assuming that with respect to any possible event, an omnipotent being would have power sufficient to determine the occurrence or nonoccurrence of that event (i.e., complete control). What we would like to know is whether it would make sense to suppose that some other agent could also have some control with respect to some selection of worldly events. It is to this problem that I now turn attention.

Look closely at this diagram:

Fig. 4: Over-Power

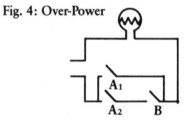

Here, the circuit represented has three switches instead of two. Switch A^1 is located on the wire pictured in the middle of the diagram and switches A^2 and B are mounted on the wire portrayed at the bottom. The circuit as a whole might best be thought of as a complex consisting of the situations portrayed in Fig. 1 and Fig. 2 taken together. There is a parallel subcircuit consisting of the wires represented by the middle and bottom lines and there is also a series circuit set up on the bottom line alone. Now suppose that there are just two agents—Bailey who is in position to work switch B and Arthur who is stationed between A^1 and A^2 and can thus operate both of them at once. We can see right away that Arthur has complete control with respect to E. He has full positive control because if he closes A^1 (A^2 either open or closed) the light goes on. He also has full negative control because if he opens A^2 while holding A^1 open, the light goes off. The question before us, then, is whether, and if so what, power can be assigned to Bailey in this situation.

Arthur announces that on Monday one or both of his switches will be *fixed* for the whole day. To say that a switch is "fixed" is to say that its operator has put the switch into a given position and then has removed his hand and assumed a posture of rest with respect to its operation. There are a number of switch arrangements that might be considered. I shall deal with only four.

Arrangement 1: Arthur fixes A^2 in the open position. On Monday, Bailey is then by-passed as he was in the situation represented in Fig. 3. Bailey has no control. Arthur retains complete control *via* his other switch, A^1.

Arrangement 2: Arthur fixes A^2 in the closed position. Since the flexible part of the circuit portrayed in Fig. 4 is now the parallel subcircuit governed by A^1 and B, it would seem reasonable to suppose that on Monday Bailey acquires the same complex of powers he has in the situation pictured in Fig. 1. Assuming that this is right, on Monday Bailey has full positive control and partial negative control with respect to E. This is because with A^2 fixed in a closed position, Bailey has power sufficient to affect E (by closing B), and he also has power so to act as to provide a necessary condition for not-E (B open). But now if we allow this, though nothing changes as regards Arthur's full positive control, what shall we say about Arthur's full negative control? Should we conclude that on Monday it is no longer his since, on Monday, Bailey has partial negative control? I think not. We have supposed that Arthur has closed A^2 and has assumed a posture of rest with respect to its operation. But this is not to suggest that he has left his station, paralyzed his hand, or in some way lost his *ability* to operate A^2. By hypothesis, on Monday Arthur is keeping A^2 closed, but he *could* open it. He still has *power* sufficient to effect not-E. The right conclusion would thus appear to be that in this situation Arthur still has full negative control even though Bailey has acquired partial negative control. But, of course, this sounds paradoxical. It is to say that on Monday Arthur has power *sufficient* to effect not-E, and yet that on Monday Bailey has power to act so as to provide a necessary condition for not-E. However, paradox does not really threaten. We can straighten it out if we make explicit a distinction which is already built into the situation. Bailey's partial negative control is *conditioned* in the sense that it is his only because and only as long as A^2 is fixed in the closed position. Arthur's full negative control is not conditioned in this sense. It is his whether or not any of the switches pictured in Fig. 4 are actually open or closed. The full description, then, is that on Monday Arthur has full *unconditional* negative control (as he always did) and, on Monday, Bailey has partial and *conditional* negative control with respect to E. We might put this so: On Monday, by closing A^2 and assuming a posture of rest with respect to its operation, Arthur *delegates* but does not thereby *lose* some negative control to Bailey. On Monday, *by Arthur's leave,* Bailey has partial negative control (and, for that matter, full positive control) with respect to E.

Arrangement 3: Arthur fixes A^1 in the open position. In this circumstance, the flexible part of the complex pictured in Fig. 4 is the series subcircuit governed by switches A^2 and B. We are thus prompted to say that on Monday Bailey acquires the cluster powers he has in the circumstance represented in Fig. 2, *viz.,* full negative control and partial positive control. But, again, the fact that Bailey has acquired partial positive control does not mean that Arthur has somehow lost full positive control. A^1 is open but Arthur could easily close it. This is to say that Arthur has power that he is not exercising. Paradox? No. We can sort it out as we did above. Arthur's full positive control is unconditional while Bailey's partial positive control (as well as his full negative control) is conditioned by the fact that Arthur is at rest with A^1 open. Bailey has been delegated power; by Arthur's leave, on Monday Bailey gets to have a say about whether the light goes on or off.

Arrangement 4: Arthur fixes A^2 in the closed position and A^1 in the open position. Bailey now assumes full positive control and full negative control, i.e., complete control with respect to E. Of course, unlike Arthur's, Bailey's complete control is conditioned. It is his only because and only as long as Arthur chooses to keep things as they are. Still, Bailey's takeover is complete. For as long as Arthur is favorably disposed, it is Bailey who actually decides whether the light goes on or off.

With A^2 fixed in the closed position, with A^1 fixed in the open position, or with A^2 fixed in the closed position and A^1 fixed in the open position, Bailey has power. In each case his power is conditional, but it would not do to say that it is illusory or in any way less than real. In all three cases, Bailey acquires the ability to make a causal contribution to the occurrence or nonoccurrence of E. However, even in the case where both Arthur and Bailey have complete control with respect to E (Arrangement 4), Arthur has a kind of dimension of control that Bailey does not have. In this situation, though both Arthur and Bailey have power sufficient to determine the condition *of the light,* Arthur has power sufficient to determine which, if any, powers Bailey shall have at any given moment. This last is what I am calling "over-power." It is the power one has when one can completely determine which, if any, powers are possessed by agents other than oneself.

Freedom Within Omnipotence

Go back for a moment to the situation pictured in Fig. 3. Here Arthur has complete control with respect to E. But that is not all. In this circumstance, Arthur not only has *power* sufficient to determine E and *power* sufficient to determine not-E, he *does in fact* determine E or he *does in fact* determine not-E. We might put this by saying that in the situation represented by Fig. 3, there is no *inefficacious position* for Arthur, i.e., there is no way to arrange things so that Arthur is not either affecting E or effecting not-E. Now, allowing "E" and "not-E" to take as values the occurrence or nonoccurrence respectively of any possible event, we emerge with Arthur as omnipotent. And what is interesting, I think, is that in this picture the omnipotent being is portrayed as one who not only has *power* to determine the occurrence or nonoccurrence of any possible event, but as one who *does in fact* determine whatever it is in the universe that actually happens. This is the way in which John Calvin understood the notion of divine omnipotence. It is a view that allows for no significant distinction between the idea of omnipotence on the one hand and the idea of active, omni-determining providence on the other.[5] Further, and with this much established, if we include the actions of created beings among the events of the world, it is a concept of omnipotence that most would regard as quite incompatible with the idea of creaturely freedom. Here, creatures not only do not control their own behavior, that behavior is completely decided by the actions of the omni-determining being. All of this is quite explicit in Calvin. In fact, the last mentioned implication is elaborated in his writings with great, indeed, bewildering abundant enthusiasm.[6]

Move now to the situation diagrammed in Fig. 4. Letting "E" and "not-E" take as values the occurrence and nonoccurrence respectively of any possible event, Arthur is again represented as an omnipotent being. But here we can make perfectly good sense of the idea that there are events that the omnipotent being neither determines to occur nor determines not to occur. In Fig. 4 there is an inefficacious position for Arthur, *viz.*, one in which he has fixed A^1 in an open position and A^2 in a closed position. What this allows us to represent is what J. L. Mackie once aptly labeled "second-order omnipotence," i.e., the power to determine that others shall determine some selection of worldly events.[7] This is what I am calling "over-power." But with this included as part of our notion of omnipotence, even if we allow the actions of finite agents to be numbered among the events of the world, there is no reason to deny that creatures have freedom in the theistic universe. All we need add is that their individual actions are among those events that the omnipotent being leaves for creatures to determine for themselves.

Urban and Walton tell us that if God has power sufficient to determine the occurrence or nonoccurrence of any possible event, then God "has all the power in the universe leaving no room for other centers of power." If God has complete control with respect to the occurrence of every possible event, then creatures have no control, even with respect to their own behavior. But while there is a way of understanding the notion of omnipotence that does at least seem to deliver this conclusion (Calvin's), there is an alternative conception that seems equally clear to avoid it. The latter trades on the possibility that God has power that he does not exercise but delegates to others to exercise instead. Calvin rejected this last-mentioned thesis. He maintained that those who exploit it in their theological systems are "sophists" really committed to deny that God has complete control with respect to worldly events.[8] This is contrapositive (and is thus the equivalent) of the reasoning employed by Urban and Walton as well as Flew and Griffin when deriving behavioral determinism from the doctrine of divine control. But the hiatus, I think, is manifest. As with one's power, one's control can extend further than one's actual determinations—as, for example, a government commission might have complete control over the price of gasoline and yet be content (for as long as they cooperate) to let individual oil companies set the actual price per gallon. The key, I think, lies in the notion of over-power. If it is coherent (as I think it is), there can be creaturely freedom within the scope of divine omnipotence.

St. Thomas on Free Will and Evil

In Pt. I-II, Q. 79, a. 1 of the *Summa Theologica*, St. Thomas Aquinas addresses the question of whether God is the cause of sin. Most of his response to this enquiry is contained in the following excerpt:[9]

> I answer that man is in two ways a cause either of his own or of another's sin. First, directly, namely by inclining his or another's will to sin; secondly, indirectly, namely by not preventing someone from sinning...Now God cannot be directly the cause of sin, either in Himself or in another, since every sin is a departure from the order, which is to God as the end: whereas God inclines and turns all things to Himself as to their last end...so that it is impossible that He should be either Himself or to another the cause of departing from the order which is to Himself. Therefore He cannot be directly the cause of sin. In like manner neither can He cause sin indirectly. For it happens that God does not give some the assistance that were He to give, they would not sin. But he does all this according to the order of His Wisdom and Justice: so that if someone sins it is not imputable to Him as though He were the cause of that sin; even as the pilot is not said to cause the wrecking of the ship, through not steering the ship, unless he ceases to steer while able and bound to steer. It is therefore evident that God is nowise a cause of sin.

But it might be objected (Obj. 3):

> The cause of the cause is the cause of the effect. Now God is the

cause of free-will, which itself is the cause of sin. Therefore God is the cause of sin.

To this St. Thomas replies:

> The effect which proceeds from the middle cause, according as it is subordinate to the first cause, is reduced to that first cause: but if it proceed from the middle cause, it is not reduced to that first cause: thus if a servant do anything contrary to his master's orders, it is not ascribed to the master as though he were the cause thereof. In like manner sin, which the free-will commits against the commandment of God, is not attributed to God as being the cause.

Before proceeding, I should like to identify what I take to be the essentials of the reasoning advanced in these several passages.

Verbally, the generative question concerns the *causes* of sin. But on the interpretation that I shall assume (and, let me agree, there might be others), the real issue has less to do with establishing causes than it has with locating *responsibility*. St. Thomas assures us that although the universe contains creatures who sometimes do what is wrong, God is "nowise the cause" of this behavior. The point (I shall assume) is that this behavior is not (as he says) "imputable" to God in the sense that God is not to be held responsible for it. The argument for this conclusion can perhaps best be seen as unfolding in two broad steps.

(1) God created beings with free will, i.e., (as St. Thomas says in *Summa Theologica*, Pt. I, Q. 83) "the power to choose." (This, of course, is an exercise of over-power on God's part.) But, if creatures have the power to choose, they are then able to opt for courses of action that are forbidden by divine command. Assume that they do. These, then, are cases in which the "middle cause" (free will) is operating "outside of the order of the first cause" (contrary to God's command) and thus, although the first cause (God) is indeed the cause (creator) of the middle cause he cannot be said to be the cause, i.e., responsible for, the final effect, sin. Thomas points out that if the servant acts contrary to his master's commands, the actions of the servant cannot be "ascribed" to the master. The master, in other words, cannot be held responsible for them.

84

(2) But, it might be wondered, couldn't God step in and prevent his creatures from acting contrary to his orders? St. Thomas says that he could—he might offer what Thomas calls "assistance." But in his wisdom and justice, God often does not provide such assistance. Still, he is not responsible for the sins committed. Since creatures have been given control over their own behavior, they alone must shoulder responsibility for what they do. Thomas says that God is like the pilot of a ship that is wrecked at a time when he is not steering. He cannot be held responsible for the wreck unless it can be shown that he was both able and bound to steer. If we think of the actions of a created agent as movements of a ship under the control of an ordinary seaman rather than the pilot, then Thomas's position is that God is able to steer—through "assistance." The conclusion must be that since created agents have been given control, God is under no obligation to steer.

There is one feature of the reasoning just reviewed that seems to me to be especially insightful. I think I can best get at it by comparing St. Thomas's theodicy with the one that Alvin Plantinga has recently tried to establish as possibly true—i.e., free of contradiction—but does not himself claim to be actually correct. I'll pause for a moment to sketch the highlights of Plantinga's thinking.[10]

God can create a world in which creatures perform morally right actions only if he creates agents with free will. Unless it is performed freely, an action has no moral value (positive or negative) and thus does not qualify as morally right. But, if God creates agents with free will, he then provides the precondition for wrongdoing as well as rightdoing. And (the argument continues), God cannot provide the precondition for wrongdoing and, at the same time, prevent wrong actions from being performed. Now assume that no matter which free creatures God might create, all would opt to perform at least some immoral actions. (This last is claimed to be consistent whether or not it is actually true.) It is then not within God's power to create a world in which creatures perform morally right actions but do not also perform some actions that are wrong. God is justified in creating the present world—one containing free creatures who perform both right actions and wrong actions—because in this world there is a favorable "balance" of right action over wrong. (That there is such a balance is the second point that is claimed to be consistent but is not advanced as an actual truth.)

This argument shares two things in common with that of St. Thomas: first, its premise-set includes essential mention of creaturely free will; and, second, at bottom, it reaches the conclusion that apart from the act whereby God confers free will on creatures in the first place, God is not responsible and thus cannot be blamed for the fact that creatures perform immoral actions. However, in this theodicy, the last-mentioned conclusion is reached a little differently than it is by St. Thomas. Plantinga says that as long as men are free to perform morally right actions, not even an omnipotent being can prevent them from performing morally wrong actions. In his words: "[God] can forestall the occurrence of moral evil only by removing the possibility of moral good," i.e., only by removing free will.[11] This (presumably) logical limitation on God's power is what supports—indeed *requires*—the conclusion that apart from having provided free will in the first place, God cannot be held responsible for wrong actions. Nothing like this can be found in the passages cited above from St. Thomas. In fact, St. Thomas claims that although men have free will, it is within God's power to provide what he calls "assistance" in cases where men would otherwise do what is wrong: by way of "assistance" God could assure that no creature performs an immoral action. But, it will be objected, to "assist" creatures in the way indicated would be to *cause* them not to behave in morally objectionable ways. This, in turn, would be to deprive creatures of free will and thus to preclude not only wrong action, but the very possibility of right action as well. This objection seems clearly to turn on a mistake. Suppose that God were to provide "assistance" only when needed. At best, what follows is that men would not be free to perform a specific range of actions, *viz.*, wrong actions. But this no more implies the absence of free will than does, for example, the fact that men are not now free to hang unsupported in the atmosphere or to travel faster than the speed of light. One has free will if one is free to choose between alternatives. But this does not require that the alternatives in question be unlimited. I lock my car or leave my phone off the hook. This limits my neighbor's alternatives but it does not thereby reduce the number of free agents in the world. If God were to provide "assistance" in cases where men would otherwise do what is wrong, this would diminish men's options but

86

would in no way diminish the free population. The men "assisted" would still be free to choose among a myriad of non-wrong actions. Most importantly, the men "assisted" would still be free to perform those actions that are morally right. Analogy: The police in Sunnyville have developed a system whereby they can anticipate and prevent all instances of illegal behavior. Their techniques are action-specific, i.e., they do not employ massive prevention measures such as imprisoning the whole population or even potential lawbreakers. Citizens are free to do as they please as long as they do not attempt to break the law. Only illegal behavior is prevented—it is stopped before it can be successfully completed. It is perhaps not irrelevant to add that Sunnyville is filled with citizens of all ages who have won special awards for meritorious behavior. So far as I can see, an omnipotent (and omni-scient) being could prevent wrong action while, at the same time, allowing creatures free will and thus preserving the precondition of morally right action. Since the theodicy that Plantinga discusses depends importantly on his insistence to the contrary, that theodicy seems to me to be conceptually deficient.[12] However, in the present context, the point to be emphasized has less to do with the Plantinga reasoning than it does with the theory advanced by St. Thomas. Whatever may be our final verdict regarding the success of Thomas's theodicy, I think he was right to acknowledge at the outset that God can prevent creatures—even free creatures—from sinning. It is to his credit that he faced squarely this implication of traditional thinking about God's capabilities. I turn now to probe the rest of his thinking on this topic.

Making use of an example that is inspired by St. Thomas's analogy of the pilot, I want first to consider two fanciful situations designed to flex part of the complex web of ordinary intuitions that govern our thinking on the topic of moral responsibility. The example I have in mind is that of the automobile used in driver training programs which is equipped with what is called "dual control." In addition to the usual controls operated from the driver's side, vehicles with dual control are rigged with a functional brake peddle on the floor of the passenger's side as well as with a second ignition switch by which the in-car instructor can cut the engine at will. More sophisticated models include a steering wheel on the passenger's side. We could easily imagine an arrangement that would completely replicate the situation diagrammed in Fig. 4—two full sets of controls and a switch similar to A² by which the instructor can engage or disengage the control system operated by the trainee. The cases I want to consider are these:

Case 1: An intersection, plainly marked with a legal stop sign, is located on a practice track operated by the City of San Diego as part of its driver training program. Though the track is large and encompasses a variety of cross streets, bridges, etc., for safety reasons only one car at a time is allowed to run. Bailey (the trainee) is driving; he has been thoroughly briefed as regards traffic regulations. Arthur (the instructor) is in the passenger seat with his special ignition switch in the "on" position. He has assumed a posture of watchful rest with respect to the operation of the car. As Bailey approaches the intersection of interest, he accelerates beyond the legal speed limit. The car runs the stop sign and continues through the intersection without so much as the slightest hesitation. Throughout, Arthur makes no move to interfere. At the end of the run, Bailey is chastised for his errors and is given a failing grade on his performance for the day.

Assuming that there are no extenuating circumstances (e.g., that Bailey did not suffer an attack of narcolepsy while at the wheel), I think it is clear that Bailey is responsible for the fact that the car was travelling in excess of the speed limit and failed to stop at the intersection as required. He was cognizant, informed, and was driving the car. He was thus justly chastised and punished (in the form of the failing score) for his performance. But what about Arthur? To be sure, Bailey was driving, but Arthur could have prevented the violations. He could have hit the brake, cut the engine, or both. Maybe Arthur should be chastised and punished as well. Maybe Arthur should be chastised and punished *instead.*

Note, first of all, that were we simply interested in locating *responsibility,* the honors would probably have to be split between the two principles. With respect to the fact that the car was traveling in excess of the speed limit and failed to stop at the intersection, Bailey is responsible as doer and Arthur is responsible as permitter. Nor is this paradoxical or odd. It is a standard way of distributing responsibility both in ordinary moral contexts and in legal settings as well.[13] However, the question before us concerns *blame* and not just responsibility. And on this issue, I think that Bailey alone must accept the burden. Arthur is not to be chastised or punished. In fact, he might even be praised for his restraint and rewarded (in the form of a raise) for his patience as an instructor. After all, how is Bailey going to learn how to drive if he is never permitted to make a mistake?

Case 2: An intersection again plainly marked with a legal stop sign is located in downtown San Diego. The time is evening rush hour and the intersection is crowded with vehicles and pedestrians. Bailey is driving and as he approaches the scene, he accelerates beyond the legal speed limit and, narrowly missing the stop sign itself, careens into the busy cross street. The car hits a loaded school bus which was fully visible from the beginning and clearly had the right of way. As before, Arthur makes no effort to interfere. In the end, six children are taken to the emergency ward with broken bones and bleeding wounds. Two are dead before morning.

Again, assuming that there are no extenuating circumstances, Bailey must be assigned responsibility for the violations and the consequent tragedy. He could not plead incapacity and he was surely aware of the danger inherent in his illegal action. Blame and punishment would be fully appropriate. But what about Arthur? As in Case I, he can again be assigned responsibility—the responsibility that goes with his role as permitter. But this time the circumstances clearly indicate that he may not be just responsible, but *liable.* Look at it this way: Bailey was a trainee—inexperienced, nervous from the outset. One could expect that the prospect of negotiating a busy intersection would occasion some degree of panic. However, Arthur was the instructor—experienced and confident as a driver. Further, we might imagine that Arthur had been over the route many times with dozens of trainees. He should have anticipated the problem and been ready to act as soon as disaster began to unfold. To be sure, Bailey did it—he ran the stop sign, hit the bus, and killed the children. But the point is that although he had operational control of the vehicle, he shouldn't have had it—Arthur should have had it. Arthur had over-power. Unless there is something in the story that we have not yet been told, it would appear that it was his obligation to take control from Bailey and guide the car himself.

In the example just sketched, I have assumed that Arthur has complete control with respect to the motions of the car but not that he has complete control (or even partial control) with respect to Bailey's bodily activities, decisions, or choices. Arthur is thus responsible for the motion of the car (and its consequences), but that is as far as his responsibility is extended. However, in the case of God, the range of control broadens. Allowing that the activities (even deciding or choosing activities) of creatures can be included in the class of events, God has complete control not only with respect to the circumstances that result from the freely chosen actions of creatures, but with respect to the freely chosen actions themselves. Now, St. Thomas maintains that since creatures have been given free will and can thus be held responsible for their actions generally and for those that are contrary to divine command in particular, God is "nowise the cause," that is, is not responsible for the actions nor (presumably) for the events that issue therefrom. I think that this is a mistake even in the case where the actions of creatures have no morally relevant dimension other than the fact that they violate law. In Case 1, for example, Arthur is responsible *qua* permitter for the fact that the car is traveling in excess of the speed limit and fails to stop at the intersection as required. In this case, it is blame and not responsibility that is justly assigned to Bailey alone. Thinking of the actions of creatures as analogous to the motions of the car, even if it could be argued that God is not to be blamed for creaturely behavior that is contrary to law, that he is *responsible* for such behavior seems to me to be clear. However, where the reasoning involved in St. Thomas's theodicy goes wrong in a really salient way is where it is applied to cases in which the actions of creatures are not only contrary to divine command but result in the suffering and misery of other sentient beings. Here I might point to dramatic cases such as Auschwitz and Bangladesh—holocausts consequent on immoral actions of overwhelming magnitude. But perhaps in the long run it is the everyday tragedies that issue from commonplace offenses that are better used for illustration. It's when the kid next door is raped and strangled that attention is more likely to be peaked. Working St. Thomas's example of the disobedient servant together with that of the pilot, these are cases in which the ordinary seaman who is left to steer not only disobeys the pilot's orders, but wrecks the ship and drowns his shipmates as well. Assume now that God not only has over-power with respect to human actions, but, being omniscient, knows in advance that his commands will be violated and that suffering will be the result. The full analogy, then, is the pilot who is not only able to take over the wheel, but is fully aware that if he fails to do so his orders will be disobeyed and disaster will strike. Shall we say that since the seaman who has been given control, violates command, he is responsible and appropriately blamed for the wreck? That seems right. What would be wrong, however, is from this to conclude that in the situation imagined the pilot's responsibility ceased when he delegated control, and thus that he is not *also* responsible for the ensuing wreck. And, of course, it is the counterpart of this that constitutes the trust of St. Thomas's theodicy. It is the claim that since creatures have been given control over their own behavior, they are thus responsible for their own immoral actions. Apart from the act whereby he conferred free will in the first place (which is not here at issue), God is simply not called upon to answer. But if God has over-power, this thesis is simplistic to the point of being absurd. As long as he retains control over their powers to control their individual actions, God is not just responsible for the fact that creatures *can* sin (i.e., that they have free will), he, *as well as they,* is responsible for what they *actually do.*

Epilogue: So how shall God answer—or, better, how shall we answer for him? Note that this question becomes relevant only after we agree that the conclusion reached in St. Thomas's theodicy is false. Insofar as God is not responsible, to that extent is justification neither required nor even appropriate. But, again, how shall we answer? What is needed is easily described but may be difficult to deliver. It is a reason for thinking that when shipwreck is pending, God is not (though quite able) *himself* "bound to steer."

Augustine on Evil

In chapter 96 of the *Enchiridion,* St. Augustine writes as follows concerning the existence of evil in the theistic universe.[14]

> Nor can we doubt that God does well even in the permission of what is evil. For He permits it only in the justice of His judgment. And surely all that is just and good. Although, therefore, evil, in so far as it is evil, is not a good; yet the fact that evil as well as good exists, its existence would not be permitted by the omnipotent

God, who without doubt can as easily refuse to permit what He does not wish, as bring about what He does wish. And if we do not believe this, the very first sentence of our creed is endangered, wherein we profess to believe in God the Father Almighty. For He is truly called Almighty if He cannot do whatever he pleases, or if the power of His almighty will is hindered by the will of any creature whatsoever.

In chapter 100 of the same text, the principle enunciated in the foregoing passage is applied to the special case of immoral action:

These are the great works of the Lord, sought out according to all His pleasure, and so wisely sought out, that when the intelligent creation, both angelic and human, sinned, doing not His will but their own, He used the very will of the creature which was working in opposition to the Creator's will as an instrument for carrying out His will, the Supremely Good thus turning to good account even what is evil...For as far as relates to their own consciousness, these creatures did what God wished not to be done; but in view of God's omnipotence, they could in nowise effect their purpose. For in the very fact that they acted in opposition to His will, His will concerning them was fulfilled. And hence it is that "the works of the Lord are great, sought out according to all His pleasure", because in a way unspeakably strange and wonderful, even what is done in opposition to His will does not defeat His will. For it would not be done did He not permit it (and of course His permission is not unwilling, but willing); nor would a Good Being permit evil to be done only that in His omnipotence He can turn evil into good.

Augustine says that if a man sins, he does so by God's leave and with his permission. Since God is omnipotent and could thus readily prevent it, if he did not permit it the man simply would not succeed in sinning. Shall we then conclude that God is to be blamed for immoral actions and the shipwrecks such as Auschwitz that follow as consequences? Of course, Augustine's answer is negative. He claims that "in a way unspeakably strange and wonderful," these very evils are turned to good account. In the final analysis, whatever evils God permits (including sinful actions), make a positive contribution to the ultimate good. If they did not, God being perfectly good as well as omnipotent, simply would not allow them to occur.

This theodicy stands in contrast to the one offered by St. Thomas (as well as the one discussed by Alvin Plantinga) in at least two important ways.

First, the hinge of St. Thomas's reasoning consists in the claim that since creatures are free to either obey or disobey divine command, if they choose not to do so, they alone can be held responsible (and thus properly blamed) for their immoral actions and their untoward consequences. But this is not Augustine's view—at least not in the passages we are now considering. Here, the focus of the thinking has nothing to do with the assignment of responsibility. It consists, instead, in Augustine's evaluation of the permitted evils. The crucial claim is that immoral actions and their consequent outcomes have positive value by virtue of their contribution to the ultimate good. It is because of this, and not because he lacks responsibility for the events in question, that God is not to be blamed for their occurrence. Blame is appropriate only in cases where what is permitted has negative value. Thus, if we agree with Augustine that "the fact that evil as well as good exists is a good," to blame God for allowing evil would make no sense at all. The situation here is reminiscent of the practice-track situation where the chain between the traffic violations and Arthur's culpability is broken not at the link of responsibility but at the next one down, *viz.*, blame.

Secondly, St. Thomas's theodicy has as an essential ingredient the claim that creatures have free will. It is because of this that creatures, rather than God, are responsible for their immoral actions and the events that result. But Augustine's theodicy requires no such premise. Since the argument is not aimed at shifting responsibility away from God, it could proceed as well even if it were admitted that God *alone* is responsible for what happens, i.e., that creatures (to turn things around) are "nowise the cause." Note, I am not here suggesting that Augustine actually held this view: I suspect that if he had, it would have caused trouble elsewhere in his theology. Note, too, that Augustine's theodicy in no way precludes a doctrine of creaturely freedom and a consequent acknowledgement of creaturely responsibility. The point that I am after is as it stands and considered apart from other elements of his theology, Augustine's theodicy is independent of any assumption concerning the existence or nonexistence of creaturely freedom. This again marks a difference between his and St. Thomas's theodicy. It also provides occasion for an interesting historical observation, *viz.*, that in Pt. I, Chap. 28, Sec. 3 of the *Institutes,* Calvin cites with profound approval most of the second passage from the *Enchiridion* quoted at the beginning of this section.[15] Calvin apparently saw very clearly that unlike the one advanced by St. Thomas, Augustine's theodicy could be consistently adopted in a theological system in which it is also held that God alone determines whatever happens in the universe including the actions of creatures.

I have argued that if we think of God as having over-power, the doctrine of divine omnipotence does not conflict with the notion of creaturely freedom. I have also argued that this same assumption requires the rejection of any theodicy in which it is claimed that apart from the act whereby God confers free will to creatures in the first place, God is not responsible for the evil in the universe that consists in or results from the immoral actions of creatures. On the basis of the admittedly sketchy remarks in this last section, I now want to add that even if theodicies of this last-mentioned sort are discarded, Augustine's remains to be considered. The argument that touches the former does nothing to undermine the cogency of the latter. Further, although Augustine's stance on the problem of evil is bold, I am inclined to think that it can be formulated in a way that avoids conceptual incoherence.[16] With patient attention to the problem of identifying the good to which permitted evils ultimately contribute, it may also be capable of more specific development than Augustine himself ever attempted.[17] But whether or not either of these last speculations is right, if God has over-power, at least one negative conclusion seems to me to be in order. If there is promise of an adequate theodicy sometime in the future, it does not lie in some further effort to establish that God is not responsible for the freely performed, immoral actions of creatures.

NOTES

1 *The Power of God: Readings on Omnipotence and Evil,* ed. Linwood Urban and Douglas Walton (Oxford: Oxford University Press, 1978), 192-93.

2 Anthony Flew, *God and Philosophy* (New York: Harcourt, Brace and World, 1966), 46-47.

3 Ibid., 55-56.

4 David Griffin, *God, Power and Evil: A Process Theodicy* (Philadelphia: Westminster, 1976), chaps. 17 and 18. See also Charles Hartshorne's article "Omnipotence," in *An Encyclopedia of Religion,* ed. Vergilious Fern (New York: Philosophical Library, 1962); and *The Divine Relativity* (New Haven: Yale University Press, 1938), chap. 2.

5 John Calvin, *Institutes of the Christian Religion* (Grand Rapids, Mich.: Eerdmans, 1953), bk. I, chap. 16, secs. 3-4.

6 For example, see *Institutes of the Christian Religion,* bk. II, secs. 1-10 and bk. III, chap. 23, secs. 6-9.

7 J. L. Mackie, "Evil and Omnipotence," *Mind,* 1957, sec. 4. See also the third paragraph of Peter Geach's essay "Omnipotence", *Philosophy* 48 (1973), where he briefly describes what he calls God's "Almightiness" or "power over all things." Incidently, I shall not here deal with Mackie's claim that a single being cannot have unlimited first order omnipotence and unlimited second order omnipotence (power to determine the power of others) at the same time. For what I think is the correct reply to Mackie on this point, see Bernard Mayo's "The Paradox of Omnipotence," *Mind,* 1961.

8 Calvin, *Institutes of the Christian Religion,* bk. I, chap. 16, secs. 3-4. In sec. 4 Calvin writes: "Not so gross is the error of those who attribute governance to God but of a confused and mixed sort, as I have said, namely, one that by a general motion revolves and drives the system of the universe, with its several parts, but which does not specifically direct the action of individual creatures. Yet this error, also, is not tolerable; for by this providence which they call universal, they teach that nothing hinders all creatures from being contingently moved, or man from turning himself hither and thither by the free choice of his will. [This view, Calvin continues, takes from God] the chief thing: that he directs everything by his incomprehensible wisdom and disposes it to his own end. And so in name only, not in fact, it makes God the ruler of the universe because it deprives him of his control. What, I pray you, is it to have control but so to be in authority that you rule in a determined order those things over which you are placed."

9 St. Thomas Aquinas, *Summa Theologica,* pts. 1-2, q. 79, trans. Fathers of the English Dominican Province (New York: Bensinger Bros., 1947).

10 The following paragraph contains a summary of the argument developed by Alvin Plantinga in the first ten sections of *God, Freedom and Evil* (Grand Rapids, Mich.: Eerdmans, 1978), sec. A. Plantinga supplies his own sketch of the argument on pages 30-31.

11 Plantinga, *God, Freedom and Evil*, 30. The whole passage reads as follows: "To create creatures capable of moral good...[God] must create creatures capable of moral evil; and he can't give these creatures the freedom to perform moral evil and at the same time prevent them from doing so. As it turns out, sadly enough, some of the free creatures God created went wrong in the exercise of their freedom; this is the source of moral evil. The fact that free creatures sometimes go wrong, however, counts neither against God's omnipotence nor against His goodness; for he could have forestalled the occurrence of moral evil only by removing the possibility of moral good."

The conclusion is, then, that although God is omnipotent, he *could not* create a world in which creatures perform right actions (which requires free will) without creating a world in which creatures also perform immoral actions. Plantinga adds that the "heart" of his own position (formulated in what he calls the "Free Will Defense") is that this conclusion is "possible," i.e., free of contradiction. As Plantinga moves into the technical development theodicy just sketched in "preliminary" fashion, the idea that God is powerless to prevent free creatures from performing immoral actions is advanced in conjunction with a doctrine referred to as "transworld depravity." Though it is too complex to present in even a cursory manner here, those familiar with this part of Plantinga's reasoning will find the theme in which I am presently interested clearly stated at the end of sec. A, subsec. 7 of *God, Freedom and Evil*, 53, where Plantinga writes:

"But if every essence suffers from transworld depravity, then no matter which essences God instantiates, the resulting persons, if free with respect to morally significant actions, would always perform at least some wrong actions. If every essence suffers from transworld depravity, then it was beyond the power of God Himself to create a world containing moral good but no moral evil. He might have been able to create worlds in which moral evil is very considerably outweighed by moral good, but it was not within his power to create worlds containing moral good by no moral evil—and this despite the fact that He is omnipotent."

12 I developed this point a little differently in an earlier article entitled "Plantinga on Free Will and Evil," *Religious Studies*, 1979, sec. 5.

13 As regards the latter, the idea that there is permitter as well as doer responsibility is the major ingredient in the principle of *respondeat superior* ("let the master answer") which affirms, in effect, that a person is responsible for the actions of others who are (or ought to be) under that person's control, e.g., one's employees. Cf. any good legal dictionary under the heading of "Agency."

14 These passages are taken from vol. 1 of *The Basic Writings of Augustine*, ed. W. J. Oats (New York: Random House, 1948), which, in turn, were taken from *A Select Library of the Nicene and Post-Nicene Fathers of the Church*, ed. Philip Schaff (Grand Rapids, Mich.: Eerdmans, 1960).

15 See also Calvin's *Institutes*, chap. 17, secs. 5 and 11.

16 See sec. 2 of my "Hume on Evil," *Philosophical Review*, 1963. See especially Roderick Chisholm's splendid development of this idea in "The Defeat of

Good and Evil," *Proceedings of the American Philosophical Association*, 1968-69.

17 What has come to be known as the "soul-making" theodicy specifies the ultimate good as (what might be called) "spiritual maturity" which includes certain virtuous dispositions as forbearance and steadfastness. The argument is that evil in the world is logically indispensable for the ultimate good. In effect, the soul-making theodicy asks us to think of the world as a kind of training ground, a practice track of the sort described in Case 1 above. On this view, Case 2 is then not really different than Case 1. God permits both the legal violations and their consequences because they are required as part of the soul-making process. I think one can see in this a more specific version of the sort of reasoning Augustine introduces. And while I do not care to claim that it is actually successful, it does suggest that Augustine's theodicy may be capable of more concrete development. For details on the soul-making theodicy, see John Hick's *Evil and the God of Love* (New York: Harper & Row, 1966), pts. 3 and 4. See also Clement Dore's "An Examination of the 'Soul-Making' Theodicy," *American Philosophical Quarterly*, 1970.

The Feminine Image of God in Shusaku Endo

Jean Higgins

S husaku Endo has been for many years a best-selling novelist in Japan. Both his name and his novels are gradually becoming well-known in the English-speaking world as well. Four novels,[1] one play,[2] a life of Jesus,[3] and several short stories,[4] have been translated into English, and feature articles have been devoted to his work in *Time* and *Newsweek*.

Endo's work has broad appeal. It will stand on its own as good creative writing. Scholars or students in the History of Christian Thought will find his historical novels, *Silence* and *Samurai*, provocative supplementary reading to the history of the missions in the Far East in the late sixteenth and early seventeenth centuries. Those engaged in cross-cultural religious studies will be interested in his project of translating the Western Christian image of God into an image acceptable to the Japanese. The ecumenical importance of his work on the world scene is obvious. If Endo's work is successful, bridges will have been built not only between a religion and a people, but among some of the world's religions as well.

Shusaku Endo is himself a Christian, a Catholic. He was baptized at the age of eleven on the occasion of his mother's conversion. His own conversion, he makes clear, was neither an informed nor a personal choice.[5] He became a Christian because his mother wished it. Much of his work is an attempt to come to grips with that conversion. Speaking of some other Japanese novelists who became converts to Christianity as adults, Endo says:

> If I may compare this to getting married, these writers have a love of marriage in the sense that each one chose his own wife. In my case, however, it is as though I married the girl my parents chose for me when I was still a child.

> Or to change the analogy, my friends ordered their suits tailor-made; I put on a ready-made suit—unaltered—that my mother bought me. My ready-made suit did not fit. It was too long in some places, too short in others, too loose here and there. That suit and my body were mismatched, and from a certain age this bothered me all the time.[6]

As a young man, Endo was awarded a scholarship to study in France. One of the first post-war students to study abroad, he arrived in France at a time when Japan and France had no formal peace treaty. Politically and culturally he was an alien: no Japanese embassy, no Japanese colleagues, "no opportunity to see the face of a fellow countryman."[7] In France, with a "Japanese body" and a "ready-made Western religious suit," Endo found himself immersed in a culture thoroughly permeated by Christianity. He set himself to work attempting to harmonize his Japanese cultural heritage and his Western culture religion. His area of study was the creative writings of twentieth-century French Catholic novelists, many of whom claimed to be converts. In their conversion accounts, he sought some expression of the alienation he, as a convert, felt. But he found none. Endo writes:

> [T]hat implied to me, that they had returned to Christianity as to their own homeplace. But I myself had no such feeling; Christianity to me was not a journey home. Nowhere in those authors I studied did I discover what I felt: the anguish of an alien.[8]

Awareness of his own special problem of alienation led him to his choice of profession:

> From that time I began to think about becoming a novelist, for I had discovered my unique theme to pursue throughout life. And

what was that theme? It was how to make faraway Christianity something close. It was retailoring with my own hands the Western suit my mother had put on me, and changing it into a Japanese garment that would fit my Japanese body.[9]

Endo set about solving the problem (for himself and his fellow Japanese) by reinterpreting the image of God in Christ. He did this in novel form in *Silence,* in biographical form in *A Life of Jesus,* in semi-autobiographical form in the short story, "Mothers."[10] The crucial article, "The Anguish of an Alien," relates these works to his personal and professional development from his involuntary conversion, through his adult acceptance of Christianity, to his defining of his quest to bridge the gulf between the "father-religion" of Western culture and the "mother-religion" of Japan.

I began to feel that the gulf I had long felt between Christian-ity and me was due to European overemphasis on the paternal aspect of religion. Christianity seemed distant to us Japanese because the other aspect, maternal religion, had been grossly neglected from the time of the early Christian missionaries down to the present.[11]

In what follows I shall treat of the image of God in the first four of these writings, beginning with the fullest development of this theme in *A Life of Jesus.*

Endo's starting point in this portrait of Jesus is Jesus' own image of God. According to Endo, Jesus developed that image in contrast to the image of God preached by John the Baptist and common among the Jews of that period.[12] Jesus comes to conceive God as Love. He undertakes himself to preach "the love of God and the God of love."[13] But preaching a God of love—and nothing else but—turns out to involve more than a change from the Baptist's God of stern judgment and punishment. It is also a break with the God who appears in many threatening passages in the Old Testament prophets as well as in much of the popular apocalyptic material between the Testaments.[14] But just as seriously, the preaching of "the love of God and the God of love" flies in the face of simple observation of normal life. The world is filled with suffering, and God does nothing about it. How can he be a God of love? What kind of love might this be?

Jesus, in Endo's story, grows up a very sensitive and very perceptive young man. He sees the human suffering all around him. He appreciates its depth in every single person he meets. Yet, alone in the desert after a period of discipleship under John the Baptist, he has had profound personal relations with the God of love. He burns with the desire and need to make that God known. But he wonders how he can make the reality of a God of love vivid and plausible to those who suffer so long as they remain in their suffering.[15]

Western accounts of Jesus often stress that Jesus does all he can to alleviate sufferings, especially by his healings. But Endo finds equally striking in the gospels many instances when Jesus does not work a physical healing but merely offers the consolations of his attention, his presence, and his love (e.g., the woman who was a sinner in Luke 7:36-50). In others again, he notes, Jesus does heal, but the reality of consolation offered by Jesus' presence and love is as impressive in the story as the miracle itself (e.g., the woman with the issue of Blood in Mark 5:25-34).[16]

At the same time, Jesus protests against the demands made on him for ever more miracles, more healings, more visible signs (John 4:48). Moreover, on the evidence of the Gospels themselves, no matter how many people Jesus did heal, the number of those with whom his power never made contact must have been greater still. Think of all the people in the towns in Palestine which he never visited; think of the people without faith even where he did pass (Mark 6:5-6). When he heals one out of a crowd, as at the pool of Bethesda, think of the many other sufferers lying about waiting.

Thus though Jesus in the Gospels did cure people, Endo concludes that those cures were more in the nature of signs of God's presence than they were steps in an orderly campaign for the elimination of sickness and suffering. The miraculous works Jesus performed were not his solutions to the problem of suffering. Nor was Jesus' message a promise to eliminate suffering from human life. He indeed repeated prophetically God's ancient promise of a perfect world to come, but he does not announce any program whereby this perfect world can be achieved according to strategically planned action of human beings.

What Jesus announces, according to Endo, is just his God of love. Jesus says, "Blessed are the poor, blessed are those that mourn." To make those who suffer feel loved, he tries to be with them whenever he can. He exposes himself to their misery. He lets them see that he longs to share their suffering as much as possible. This does not take the pain away. It does not change the poor into rich, the mourning into those who celebrate and rejoice. It changes them only into poor who are loved, mourners who know that someone else cares.

This was in many ways a self-defeating approach Jesus took. The boldness of his preaching and his manner of life aroused great expectations. When people sensed his universal concern, they presumed that effective relief for all their ills was now at hand. But when Jesus, preaching the love of God and the God of love, summoned his hearers to heroic love and heroic forgiveness, a chill settled on the crowd. They realized that Jesus was not, in fact, the hoped-for political messiah, that he did not, in fact, have a strategy for restoring the ancient glory of Israel. Their expectations had been in vain. Disillusioned, many turned away from this politically powerless messiah of love.[17]

Why did Jesus choose this way of acting? Granted that he did not want to be a political messiah, leading the people in revolution against Rome, could he not at least have planned and executed a more effective and general campaign against human suffering? A war on disease, a war on poverty, would not necessarily have been political. And it could have done a lot of good. It would have picked out the evils that could practically be eliminated in a reasonable amount of time and concentrated on those; then advanced to others. It would have distributed resources to where they would have done the most good. It would have concentrated on the sufferers for whom something reasonably could be done.

The way Jesus chose to follow, as Endo reads his life, was not the way of efficient, practical use of power. It was the way of love. This way attempted to face fully the whole sweep, the entire reality of all human suffering—in all its immensity and in its every single instance and embodiment—even the suffering for which no one can do anything. He wanted to offer an approach to suffering that would not have to omit any instance of suffering, any person in pain.[18] Where there was pain, there he wanted to be, consoling, loving, willing to share that pain. This would be his way of showing the truth of his own faith in the God of Love. He would bring love into every human life he could; he would make love available for every human life.

Endo's point is that in this design and in his carrying it out in the way he did, Jesus did in fact make God's love visible on earth and become himself the perfect image of the love of God and the God of love.[19] For what Jesus did is also what God does. God is there and is loving us, present in our pain and privation. We tend not to believe it, because we are not being relieved of our pain. But the truth is that we are being loved. Some day the pain will vanish and only the love will remain. Some day our poverty, mourning, meekness, hunger for justice, and all the rest, will receive their promised rewards. God's word abides: "They will be comforted"; "Theirs is the kingdom of heaven"; "They shall have their fill." But human life is a matter of enduring in the in-between time, hanging on in the waiting period—which is usually a whole life long—and continuing to believe during all that time that we are surrounded by love.

A commonsense, rational, and efficient approach says: "Let us set ourselves to eliminating those problems, pains, and evils. Let us show God's love by improving the universe he has made." There is nothing wrong with such an approach. It is not false. Work to relieve suffering does show forth the love of God.

Still, there are some problems with that way: (1) Not all suffering can ever be relieved, ever be eliminated from the earth. What then about those who are left in insoluble instances? (2) Not all cases of even soluble suffering can be reached here and now with even the available solutions. What about those who do not get reached, especially if the message of love is: Your pains will be relieved. For in fact they will not be. (3) That approach not only prefers some or gives first place (necessarily) to some over others (giving rise to the question: Where do you start?), that approach also leads logically and eventually and in many instances to subordinating some to others, exploiting some (the few) for the sake of others (the many). For the focus in that approach is on results.

Now, that is why, good as all that is, it is not the perfect reflection of God and God's love. Focus on results is, in Endo's notion, typical of the love of a father. It is practical, efficient, well-planned. It takes definite steps to a definite desirable end. It can mean punishing in order to improve, withholding love and approval in order to stimulate to a greater good. It can mean cutting, hurting, in order to heal, amputating the part, in order to save the whole. It can mean making an example of one to help many. It is conditional on success, focused on results, on achievement.

But for Endo, God's love is not like that. God's love is maternal, like the love of a mother.[20] The mother, for Endo, is the one who cares not so much about the deed as about the person. She cares about being there, present, to the suffering one she loves, to hold and embrace, even if she can do nothing more. She begs to be allowed to fall ill of the same disease, be struck with the same wounds, fall prey to the same misfortunes herself, if only the pain of her loved one can be relieved. And if this cannot be, then she still wants to remain—consoling, comforting, solacing, sharing, watching, waiting—unconditionally.

Ineffective? Yes. Inefficient? Yes. Weak? To some, yes. But loving? No one can doubt it. No matter what happens; no matter how much the evil we endure has been brought on us by our selves, our own folly, selfishness, sin; no matter the weakness, the cowardice—all is embraced. As long as she is needed, she is there with a love that can be put to any test and can never be doubted. That is, for Endo, mother-love.[21]

Jesus' life was like that. And his death supremely so. He wanted a death that would be for others and that would be a summary sharing and embracing of all the helplessness, weakness, and pain of mankind.[22] Sufferers could then tell themselves, no matter what they had to face:

> One was here before me, vulnerable, weak. And that one is still here, bearing with me, sharing with me. That one remains with me in my suffering, pain, loss; he went through this too, for me.[23] I am loved, irrespective of what is happening to me.
>
> I no longer have only to believe in God's love in the midst of my suffering. I see God's love revealed in the flesh, in this loving, sharing companion. He did this to make me believe in God's love, to make me see God's love. These ills will some day pass away and God will embrace me in pure beauty, peace and joy. But meanwhile, now, here, in the midst of them, despite my own load of guilt, God is loving me. That face I see is the face of God turned toward me. That hand I feel on mine is also God's hand.

The suffering Jesus underwent is God's suffering, the suffering of "the god of love who comes himself to experience the sorrows of mankind."[24] The suffering I myself experience, then, is not punishment, but love; not abandonment, but a very special and deep presence. Out of what some may call silence, I hear him speaking. What he says is: "I am here with you, as burden-bearer, as eternal companion."

Endo holds that Christianity was born at the moment when the disciples realized that they had betrayed Christ's love and that, despite their betrayal, that love was still there for them and always would be. That was the moment they saw in Jesus the revelation of an embracing, forgiving, maternal God. This, he says, is the kind of portrait that "a Japanese can paint with true feeling."[25] It is a portrait that speaks to the religious sensibilities of the Japanese people who "tend to seek in their gods and buddhas a warm-hearted mother rather than a stern father."[26]

Some years before A Life of Jesus, Endo set out the problem of conflicting images of God in his novel, Silence.[27] The theme of this novel, Endo says, was the "revolution from paternal religion, the change from the father-religion Christ to the mother-religion Christ in the experience of the novel's hero."[28]

The hero of Silence is Sebastian Rodrigues, a Portuguese Jesuit priest who arrives in Japan at the height of the anti-Christian persecution under the Tokugawa regime. All Christian missionaries had been expelled and forbidden reentry on pain of death. But Rodrigues comes inspired by conscience and fervor to make amends for the apostasy of another Jesuit, Christopher Ferreira. He comes also as a dedicated missionary, dreaming—in the Jesuit pattern of the Spiritual Exercises of Ignatius Loyola—of new worlds to conquer for Christ. He was motivated in this conquest by daily contemplation of the face of Jesus: "a face filled with vigor and strength,"[29] a face "resplendent with the authority of a king,"[30] "a Jesus of majesty and power, an orderly Jesus who was governed by order."[31]

This image of Christ strengthens Rodrigues in the many trials he undergoes on his journeys in western Japan. A hunted man, he hides by day and travels by night, visiting underground Christians who hide him at great peril. Some of these Christians are taken hostage, tortured, and put to death because of the priest's presence. Rodrigues wonders again and again about the silence of God, about the inactivity of God in the face of such cruel persecution. Why did God not take some action?

Eventually the priest is captured, and in prison he finally comes to know a very different image of Christ.

> It was not a Christ whose face was filled with majesty and glory; neither was it a face made beautiful by endurance of pain; nor was it a face filled with the strength of a will that had repelled temptation. The face of the man who then lay at his feet was sunken and utterly exhausted.[32]

What Rodrigues gazes on with new eyes and heightened religious sensibility is the face of Christ on the *fumie*—the bronze plaque on which Christians were required to place their bare feet as a sign of their rejection of Christianity.[33] When called upon himself to trample on the face of his God—in order to relieve from slow and terrible torture those Japanese Christians who were hanging head down over a pit of excrement—Rodrigues hears the sad-eyed Christ of the *fumie* address him: "Trample! Trample! It was to be trampled on by men that I was born into this world. It was to share men's pain that I carried my cross."[34] God had broken his silence. What Rodrigues now sees when he looks at the *fumie* is not a strong, glorious leader, but a fellow-sufferer, consumed by weakness.

The face of Jesus on the *fumie* was the same face that had understood and had compassion for Judas, telling him to do quickly that which he was about to do (John 13:27).[35] It was the same face that could love and forgive and save Judas as he loved, forgave, and saved the other cowardly disciples who, in Endo's analysis, betrayed, renounced, and denied Jesus. Peter's three denials in the Gospel are but a symbol for what they all did, saving their own lives at the expense of Jesus.[36] The face on the *fumie* is the face of Jesus in his weakness, in his failure.[37] It is the face of Jesus the burden-bearer, the companion, who shares all human failure and weakness.

To Endo, this is a much more profound insight into the ideal image Christianity proposes than any image of a Jesus who leads to victory. It was an image also known to St. Paul when he wrote of "Christ crucified, to the Jews indeed a stumbling block and to the Gentiles foolishness, but to those who are saved, both Jews and Greeks, Christ the power of God and the wisdom of God" (1 Cor. 1:23). Endo's image of Jesus bears the marks of the foolishness and vulnerability of love, but also the apparent "futility of love." Though ineffective and weak to the unseeing and the unknowing, love is yet strong as death. "Strength is made perfect in weakness" (2 Cor. 12:9); "When I am weak, then I am strong" (2 Cor. 12:10).

In *Silence* Endo shows the hero shift from goal-oriented, aggressive activity for the salvation of others, to self-sacrificing surrender out of compassionate love for others. His trampling on the *fumie,* judged by his "father-religion" confreres as apostasy, was not inconsistent with the image of God, of an apparently ineffectual Jesus whose work of redemption is love.

As the people turned away from Jesus as the ineffective one, the weak failure,[38] the Church turned away from the missionary Rodrigues when he apostasized. His fellow missionaries rejected him. But he could not be the cause of continued agony for his converts or for anyone. He could never let their misery be the means to his sanctification and glory, or even the Church's glory. Let the world, the Church, anyone at all say of him what they cared to say, think of him whatever they wished. He now knew his mission was to love. Rodrigues could see in the crushed image of Jesus that this was all God asked.

The change, Endo writes, is "the change in the hero's image of Christ..."[39] Rodrigues saw now, on the *fumie,* "an image shaped by Japanese hands. It was not the orderly, solemn, strong face he had conceived as a European, but the worn-out face of a Christ suffering as we suffer."[40] The "revolution from paternal religion to maternal religion, the change from the father-religion Christ to the mother-religion Christ in the experience of the novel's hero" had taken place.[41]

For Endo, it all turns on the face. It is the face that provides him with the "matchless opportunity to fill in the gap between the Japanese and Christianity";[42] for the worn-down countenance of Jesus on the *fumie* is, for Endo, a maternal face, the face of the Japanese mother.[43]

In his semi-autobiographical short story, "Mine," that face of "that man" (Jesus), is drawn in terms of feminine faces: the faces of the hero's wife and mother. His mother's face he remembers with a "look of suffering,"[44] unsightly with crying. His wife was not his heart's choice, but a plain looking girl, chosen "so as to spare further suffering to his dead mother with her unattractive, tearful face."[46] His wife's face he describes as "terribly weary." She is "tired-faced," "tearful-faced." Her heart was bad and sometimes her breath came in spasmodic wheezings.[47] But whenever he spoke cruelly to his wife, he perceived the exhausted face of "that man" whom he had reviled time and again. Just as he had not chosen his wife out of pure love, so had he lovelessly entered into vows with "that man" (at his baptism). Like his wife, "that man" had "been his companion for thirty long years, panting with a stricken heart, bearing a homely face."[48] Just as his wife did when he spoke cruelly to her, so "that man" too was "silently watching him, all the time tears rolling down his face...which was not the splendid thing religious writers had depicted." Nevertheless, he assures "that man": "I will not desert my wife and neither will I abandon you. Inasmuch as I have tormented her I have done the same to you...But I will never, never forsake you!"[49]

In his autobiographical short story, "Mothers," Endo's mother's face, lying in death with pain written across it, is remembered as in life. But it is reshaped in terms of a statuette of Mary, cracked, half-melted, abused. That face is also the face of someone who sits at his hospital bedside when memories of long months in the hospital return to him in dreams.[50] His mother is there, holding his hand—although in fact his mother had not been at the hospital— she was already dead. That face of the one present at his bedside, the one whom he felt as his mother, he later identifies in waking hours as the distorted image of Mary on the statuette he had picked up in his mother's room after her death and had cherished ever since. The tortured face on the statue, the result of the many physical mishaps which the statue had undergone, somehow contained the essential look of his own, suffering, loving mother.[51]

Years later, however, in an expedition that was part of background research for the novel Silence, Endo visited a village and community of the kakure, the secret Christians who had survived centuries of persecution. After at least partially gaining the confidence of these harassed and frightened people, he was allowed finally to see one of the central objects of their veneration. It was kept in a hidden shrine in a small cottage belonging to the person who had been elected to play the priest's role, the religious leader of their community.[52] The painting he was shown was of the Virgin Mary, done generations ago by one of the *kakure* in memory of religious images originally imported from Europe. But his model for this painting must have been one of their own *kakure* women, at least it looked just like a mother whom Endo had seen holding a child as he made his way up to the mountain village.

There on the painting was the same sadness, fear, suffering, endurance. The face of Mary was his mother's face. It was the face of that constant presence which had pulled him through his long illness. And it was again, the face of "that man," the same sad, tortured face which the hero of *Silence* found on the *fumie* he trampled out of love.

Endo is drawn again and again to reflection on the long-term fate of these secret Christians who chose to serve Christ by denying him, preserve the Christian faith in Japan by committing public apostasy.[53] They kept the faith alive at terrible personal expense. Their clergy were eliminated. They were without the official sacraments of the Church. And every year the public ceremony of apostasy had to be repeated in front of state officials. Year after year they had to defile the image of Christ by stepping on the *fumie* with their bare feet.

Each year, after performing the required act of desecration, these secret Christians returned to their own villages and flogged themselves severely and at length for having committed so great a sin.[54] For over two hundred years, the faith was handed on, at the expense of this repeatedly renewed, formal public renunciation of Christ.

By the time the nineteenth-century missionaries made contact with them, their expression of the Christian faith had changed its emphasis. They had developed basically a maternal religion. Their prayers, rituals, and teachings now centered around the figure of the mother. Endo attributes this to the fact of their annual (or even constant) sin as a community. The shame, guilt, and disgrace they felt for continually denying God and denying what they themselves were, led them to place undue emphasis on forgiveness and mercy.[55] They sought an intercessor who would understand. They sought acceptive love, which they spontaneously associated with a mother. Gradually, the mother figure of Christianity, Mary, merged with the oriental goddess of mercy and compassion, Kwannon, to become the central figure of their devotion: Marykwannon.[56]

What they were in need of was an absolute readiness to forgive. Only in her, in the mother, did they feel they could find it. It had to be absolute readiness for absolute forgiveness for the greatest of crimes—betrayal, denying the faith. The Christ of the Gospels had said clearly and unmistakeably, "Whoever denies me before men, I also will deny him before my Father who is in heaven" (Matt. 10:33).[57] They also needed a forgiveness that was endlessly repeatable—something that they felt could only be expected of a mother. Teachings on the "father God" brought to Japan by the missionaries "came to be replaced by what is most essential in Japanese religion, devotion to Mother."[58]

Endo shares the *kakure* sentiments with respect to mother-religion.

> To me there are two kinds of religion. Erich Fromm called them father-religion and mother-religion. In father-religion, God is to be feared; he judges and punishes man's sins: he gets angry.

> Mother-religion is different. God is to man what a mother is to a bad child. God forgives; God suffers with man. As it is written in the *Tannisho*, if the righteous are saved, how much more the wicked.[59]

Therefore, what impresses Endo most in the New Testament is

> the presence of a God who suffers with us, the form of Christ who comes running to the worthless and the weaklings and bears half their suffering—the same form that is seen in a mother.[60]

He is convinced that the Japanese must be shown this image of the mother in the Christian religion. Therefore, he tried in *A Life of Jesus*

> not so much to depict God in the father image that tends to characterize Christianity but rather to depict the kind-hearted maternal aspect of God revealed to us in the personality of Jesus.[61]

111

How is one to appraise Endo's vision? First of all, the success of his cultural adaptation of Christianity to the Japanese mind is hardly for Westerners to judge. We can at most identify some objective Buddhist and Taoist analogies to some of the themes he finds most impressive in Christianity; for instance, the *hotoke* who walks and weeps with the pilgrim on life's way; the *hotoke* as supporting companion who, while sharing the suffering, takes no action to lighten the burden but enlightens the bearer; echoes of the Buddhist 'empty-nothingness'; the 'yielding' and 'passivity' usually attributed to Taoism and Pure Land Buddhism; the Buddha "who forgives everything"; the compassionate mother-love of Kwannon.[62] Endo does not claim that these are his sources, but it is likely that the echo of traditional religious themes makes his presentation of Christianity more attractive to a Japanese audience.

Secondly, Western readers can and must distinguish between what is a particular cultural adaptation and what is substantive interpretation of Christianity in Endo's work. In the main, he speaks mostly of the first; but any serious reader soon perceives that his interpretation of Christianity is not mere window-dressing, "packaging," public relations between himself and the non-Christian Japanese. He may have worked out his notion of Christianity while attempting to account for his personal situation, but he clearly believes he has discovered something authentic, of general validity, of value for all. He says, modestly enough, that the portrait he sketches is "more than the subjective, individual view of the writer."[63] But clearly he feels he has given the most plausible explanation of the founding events of the Christian religion.

His presentation of his case involves a very selective use of the New Testament texts and an interpretation which must fill in from behind the scenes of the Gospel accounts. But the Western reader who notes the presence of these devices will also be made aware that all modern Western interpretations of the New Testament are also based on selective handling of the texts. Western interpreters bring to their task the heavy weight of centuries of European culture. Readers of Endo realize anew that none of us comes to the Gospel text as a neutral observer. We always drag our own cultures and histories behind us.

Within Endo's substantive interpretation of Christianity, again we must distinguish the reality about which he speaks from the language in which he expresses it. When he says that Christianity is about Jesus as patient sufferer, burden-bearer, eternally waiting presence, endlessly forgiving love, it is hard to deny that he is pointing to fundamental features of New Testament teaching. But Endo is not the first to point to them.

Again, when Endo concludes that if these are characteristics of Jesus, then they are also attributes of God, he performs a justifiable, logical deduction which merely takes seriously the Christian doctrine that Jesus is the incarnation of God and the revelation of God *par excellence:* "No one has ever seen God; the only-begotten Son, who is in the bosom of the Father, he has revealed Him" (John 1:18). "He who has seen me has seen the Father" (John 14:9).

True, Western theologians do not typically include 'patient suffering' and 'burden-bearing' among attributes of God. They find them hard to reconcile with the *philosophia perennis.* Moreover, Western theologians temper 'endlessly forgiving love' with immediate reference to divine justice, and 'eternally waiting presence' is shorn of all passivity. But if theologians (with catechists and preachers in their train) have failed to include these among aspects of divinity, at least the mystics have not failed. Endo has a long list of predecessors among the classics of Western mysticism and spirituality.[64]

But here, finally, two critical observations must be made about the language in which Endo expresses his substantial insights. First, Endo describes the essence of his image of God as distinctly feminine. Here a doubt must be raised. To see women as especially patient sufferers, burden-bearers, eternally waiting presences, endlessly forgiving lovers, may reflect Endo's own experiences of women, but they are obviously culturally conditioned experiences. Perhaps the Japanese mother he knew, and most or even all other Japanese mothers, are in fact like that or believe they should be like that to fulfill their proper roles. But if so, they express thereby an aspect of Japanese culture. Modern American feminists do not particularly welcome the term 'feminine' for this list of attributes. Those attributes may be a part of the Christian revelation of God, but in daily life women have too often met them as negative stereotypes used exploitatively.

The second observation has to do with the way Endo usually speaks of his problems with "Christianity." If the arguments of this article are correct, what Endo really intends to criticize is only "the dominant Western image of Christianity since late medieval and Renaissance times." On the other hand, authentic and original Christianity, as he understands it, turns out to be thoroughly acceptable to him, and he proposes and advocates it not only for the Japanese, but for all his readers.

NOTES

1 *Silence (Chinomoku),* trans. William Johnston (Tokyo: Sophia-Tuttle, 1969); *The Sea and the Poison (Umi to dokuyakyu),* trans. Michael Gallagher (London: Peter Owen, 1972); *Wonderful Fool (Obaka san),* trans. Francis Mathy (London: Peter Owen, 1974); *Samurai* (New York: Harper & Row, 1982).

2 *The Golden Country (Ogon no kuni),* trans. Francis Mathy (Tokyo: Tuttle, 1970). This play deals with the same subject matter as *Silence.*

3 *A Life of Jesus (Iyesu no Shogai),* trans. Richard A. Schuchert (New York: Paulist Press, 1973).

4 "Mine" ("Watakushi no mono"), trans. Peter W. Schumacher, in *The Japan Christian Quarterly,* Fall 1974: 205-13; "Mothers" ("Haha naru mono"), trans. Francis Mathy, in *The Japan Christian Quarterly,* Fall 1974: 186-204; "Name Plates at the Crossroad" ("Fuda no Tsuji"), trans. Frank Hoff, in *Solidarity: Current Affairs, Ideas and the Arts,* July/August 1976: 63-72.

5 "The Anguish of an Alien" ("Ihōjin no kunō"), 179. This article was the lead-off essay in *The World of Shusaku Endo,* a special issue of the literary magazine *Shinpyo* (December 1973). It appeared in *The Japanese Christian Quarterly* in its Fall 1974 issue.

6 Ibid.

7 Ibid., 180.

8 Ibid., 179-80.

9 Ibid., 180.

10 Reflection on the image of the Christian God is to be found in most of Endo's works. I list here only those which will be used in this article.

11 "The Anguish of an Alien," 181.

12 *A Life of Jesus,* 24, 57.

13 Ibid., 57-58.

14 Ibid., 57.

15 Ibid., 11.

16 Ibid., 50-51.

17 Ibid., 68, 118.

18 Ibid., 48, 51.

19 "But Jesus...is the symbol of love—nay, the very incarnation of Love." (p. 147); cf. *Silence,* 248.

20 *A Life of Jesus,* 25; "The Anguish of an Alien," 182.

21 *A Life of Jesus,* 80; "The Anguish of an Alien," 181.

22 *A Life of Jesus,* 147.

23 "The Anguish of an Alien," 181; *Silence*, 244.

24 *A Life of Jesus*, 28.

25 "The Anguish of an Alien," 182.

26 *A Life of Jesus*, 1.

27 In the opinion of Graham Greene, *Silence* is "one of the finest novels of our time." (Jacket, Taplinger ed.)

28 "The Anguish of an Alien," 181.

29 *Silence*, 35.

30 Ibid.

31 "The Anguish of an Alien," 181.

32 *Silence*, 264.

33 The *fumie* could bear either the image of Christ or of the Virgin and Child.

34 *Silence*, 259.

35 *A Life of Jesus*, 119.

36 Ibid., 166f.

37 Ibid., 147.

38 Ibid., chap. 7: "Jesus the Ineffectual."

39 "The Anguish of an Alien," 181.

40 Ibid.

41 Ibid.

42 Ibid.

43 Referring to a reviewer of *Silence*, Endo writes: "The person who saw my theme clearly was Mr. Jun Eto. This critic said in his review, 'The face of Jesus on the *fumie* is the mother's face in Japan. I know nothing of Mr. Endo's personal experience with his mother, but their relationship is depicted in Jesus' face on the *fumie*.' "The Anguish of an Alien," 181.

44 "Mine," 208.

45 Ibid., 211.

46 Ibid., 211-12.

47 Ibid., 210.

48 Ibid., 212.

49 Ibid., 212-13.

50 Endo has undergone a number of operations and has spent many months recuperating in hospitals.

51 "Mothers," 200-201.

52 Ibid., 203.

53 Ibid., 198.

54 Ibid., 199.

55 The significance of shame in Japanese culture should be borne in mind here.

56 "Mothers," 200.

57 This, for the *kakure,* was the image of the 'father-religion' in Jesus.

58 "Mothers," 203.

59 "The Anguish of an Alien," 181. It might be appropriate to recall here the old Japanese saying that the four most awful things on earth are earthquakes, thunderbolts, fires, and fathers.

60 Shusaku Endo, "Concerning the novel 'Silence,'" in *The Japanese Christian Quarterly,* Spring 1970: 103.

61 *A Life of Jesus,* 1.

62 It is not without significance that the goddess Kwannon (Kuan Yin) was originally a masculine Indian deity who became feminine in the course of transmigration to the Far East.

63 "The Anguish of an Alien," 182.

64 There is a growing body of literature on the use of feminine imagery to describe God in the works of a good many mystics and spiritual writers. Patristic and medieval references would include Clement of Alexandria, John Chrysostom, Anselm of Canterbury, Bernard of Clairvaux, Francis of Assisi, Gertrude the Great, Mechtilde of Magdeburg, Juliana of Norwich, Margery Kempe, and Catherine of Siena. Post-medieval references can be found in John of the Cross, Jakob Boehme, and Mother Ann Lee.

PART TWO

God and Temporality: A Heideggerian View

Eugene T. Long

The history of Western religious thought is in part a history of efforts to conceive God using terms drawn from human experience which are stretched in symbolic or analogical talk to give expression to the experience of God as somehow both immanent and transcendent. And, because God is understood to be the ground of man's ultimate concern, much of this talk has been founded on the highest reality known to man, namely, human existence. The use of human or personal attributes in talking of God has a long history in the West, but talk of God as a person or of the personality of God is of relatively recent origin.[1]

Talk of God modelled on talk of human persons has the advantage that it seems to conform in many ways to the more personalistic understanding of God as portrayed in the biblical sources. And as Paul Tillich has said, "Man cannot be ultimately concerned about anything that is less than personal."[2] However, much of this talk has been based on a dualistic understanding of persons which has dominated much of the history of Western thought since the time of Plato. This has led to a conception of God as a completely perfect personal being, invisible, bodiless, and intangible, who created the world, exercises governance over it, and intervenes on occasions. God is separated from and set over against the world and when this is combined with an emphasis on the infinite qualitative difference between God and man, God turns out to be timeless, lifeless, and irrelevant to a world in which confidence in the capacity of sciences to explain the world has grown. In an ironic sense, talk of God based on talk of human persons has resulted in a denial of the personal in God. God appears to be a cause severed from all real relations with its effect. God becomes less than what we think of today as personal.

This result of efforts to talk of the personality of God can be explained in part by our failure to keep up with the changes that have been taking place in our way of talking about persons. Philosophers from many traditions have argued in recent years that the dualistic model for talking about persons is incoherent and does not do justice to the psychosomatic unity of persons. In some cases this has led to efforts to reduce talk of persons to physicalistic or behavioristic terms, although in many of these cases something of a transcendent dimension in persons remains permitting us to distinguish persons from nonhuman entities. The essential point is that twentieth-century thinkers are more likely to talk of a unity of the spiritual and the bodily than of their separation.

It is the existentialists, however, who seem to me to have indicated the root problem in our talk of persons. Martin Heidegger and others have argued that much of our talk of persons has not treated persons as unique entities, but has tended to talk of persons on the model of impersonal entities which are essentially complete in themselves and only endure from one moment to the next. "The 'essence' of Dasein lies in its existence," writes Heidegger, and by this he means that persons are entities for whom what one is, how one is, is an issue.[3] One does not think of rocks as projecting themselves into possible ways of being. Rocks are essentially complete, changing only as a result of external causes, enduring from one moment to the next. But persons change, develop, and in some sense take time into themselves in the context of a vision that they have for the future.

When this is forgotten, and when God is talked about on the model of a person as composed of two substances, we end up with a lifeless Being existing outside of time who yet in some incoherent way is said to act on the world. Many great theologians have conceived of God as timeless, as existing outside time, and this is understandable if time is conceived as a series of nows, and being in time as merely enduring from one moment to the next. To speak of God in time in this sense would result in God's being bound by time. But to speak of God as timeless in this sense is not only incoherent, as Swinburne has argued, it removes God from the world in which we live and makes him irrelevant to our way of being in the world.[4] Further, this conception of God seems to conflict with the biblical conception of God as one who is involved in time, who acts in history.

Martin Heidegger, perhaps more than any other contemporary philosopher, has drawn our attention to the distinction between a conception of time which is applicable to things and a conception of time which is applicable to persons. And in a footnote to *Being And Time* he encourages us to make this distinction in our conception of God. He writes, "the traditional conception of 'eternity' as signifying the 'standing now' (*nunc stans*) has been drawn from the ordinary way of understanding time and has been defined with an orientation towards the idea of 'constant' presence-at-hand"; and that "If God's eternity can be 'construed' philosophically, then it may be understood only as a more primordial temporality which is 'infinite'."[5] "Temporality" may be taken to refer to the human or personal experience of time and is distinguished from the ordinary understanding of time which applies to things. Temporality or more precisely infinite temporality, not the ordinary conception of time, should be our model for understanding God's eternity.

Heidegger does not himself develop this suggestion, but he does encourage us to take the concept of temporality as applicable to persons and stretch it by the qualification of "infinite" in order to talk of God, and it is this which I will attempt to do in this essay. Schubert Ogden and Charles Sherover have made explicit references to this footnote in *Being And Time* in their efforts to talk of God, and although John Macquarrie does not make explicit reference to this footnote, he has perhaps more than anyone else developed some of the implications of this way of talking of God.[6]

The ordinary conception of time to which Heidegger refers may be called clock time. It is that understanding of time by which we regulate ourselves according to time in the use of clocks. In this understanding of time, when one says "now," one is open to the earlier, the "now no longer" and the "then," the not yet. "Time is what is 'counted'; that is to say, it is what is expressed and what we

123

have in view, even if unthematically, when the *travelling* pointer (or the shadow) is made present. When one makes present that which is moved in its movement, one says 'now here, now here, and so on'. The 'nows' are what get counted. And these show themselves 'in every now' as 'nows' which will 'forthwith be no-longer-now' and 'nows' which have 'just been not-yet now.' The world-time which is 'sighted' in this manner in the use of clocks, we call the 'now time' (*Jetz Zeit*)."[7] Heidegger traces this conception of clock time to Aristotle and argues that it is this conception which has since Aristotle dominated the discussion of time.

Entities, including persons, when conceived under this conception of time, may be said to be in time and to endure from this time to that time. In the strict sense there is no beginning and no end to time but only an unending series of nows. There is, of course, an appropriate use of time in this sense. Rocks and trees may be said to endure from one now to the next, and even persons when talked about from an external point of view may be said to endure through a series of nows. However, persons, unlike rocks and trees, seem also to be involved in time at another level. Persons may be said to gain time, to lose time, to be ahead of time. And according to Heidegger, clock time is derivative from this more personal or experiential conception of time which he calls temporality.

> Temporality is the reason for the clock. As the condition for the possibility that a clock is factically necessary, temporality is likewise the condition for its discoverability. For while the course of the sun is encountered along with the discoveredness of entities within-the-world, it is only by making it present in awaitingly retaining, and by doing so in a way which interprets itself, that dating in terms of what is ready-to-hand environmentally in a public way, is made possible and is also required.[8]

"Temporality" then refers to the primordial conception of time which is applicable to human beings, but this conception of time gets covered up or leveled off when we conceive of human beings in terms applicable to nonhuman entities. This results, argues Heidegger, from an inauthentic mode of existing in which persons flee in the face of their end time (death) and look for more time. Time in this case becomes public time, time that belongs to all and hence to no one in particular. Heidegger does not reject the place and usefulness of the ordinary conception of time, but he does argue against the tendency to treat it as normative.

> *The ordinary representation of time has its natural justification...*
> This interpretation of time loses its exclusive and preeminent justification only if it claims to convey the "true" conception of time and to be able to prescribe the sole possible horizon within which time is to be interpreted.[9]

How then are we to understand temporality, this more primordial conception of time which is applicable to our talk of persons and from which the ordinary conception of time is derived? It is well-known that human existence of Dasein is distinguished by Heidegger from other entities. The subsistence of Dasein, he says, is not based on the substantiality of a substance but on the " '*Self-subsistence*' of the existing Self, whose Being has been conceived as Care."[10] And the ontological meaning of Care is said to be temporality. If then we are to understand temporality, we need to understand the Self or Dasein as Care and show how its possibilities of being are grounded in temporality.

Being-in-the-world is, according to Heidegger, a fundamental characteristic of Dasein. This means that Dasein is not a mere thinking subject but an embodied existence. To be in the world in this sense is not merely to take up space as an object in the world. It is to be related to the world, to be bound up or concerned with it in its activities as creating, enjoying, etc. The self or Dasein is characterized in terms of its possible ways of being in the world and these possibilities are analyzed by Heidegger in terms of a threefold structure which he calls possibility, facticity, and falling. Using these terms he is indicating that Dasein is in some sense ahead of itself, projecting its possibilities (possibility), that Dasein is not *de novo,* that it is already there, thrown into a world (facticity) and that is absorbed in its world (falling). This threefold structure, which is said to characterize the Being of everyday Dasein, is called Care and the ontological meaning of Care as we have said is temporality. The temporality of Care is shown in that as possibility Dasein is futural, ahead of itself. How it will be in the future, its way of being is an issue for it. As factical, Dasein is past, not merely, however, as no longer present at hand. Dasein *is* as already having been. And as falling, Dasein is present. That is, Dasein is present in the sense of fleeing from the future and the resolute projection of its possibilities. As present it falls into irresoluteness and avoids the issue of its way of being-in-the-world.

It should be clear that in talking of the temporal structure of Dasein as Care, Heidegger is not speaking within the framework of the ordinary conception of time. He is not suggesting, for example, that the "future" or "ahead of" means merely "in advance of something" or that "already having been" means merely "no longer now." This would be to conceive Dasein on the model of mere things or objects as enduring through a series of nows. "Temporalizing," writes Heidegger, "does not signify that ecstasies come in a 'succession.' The future is *not later* than having been, and having been is *not earlier* than the Present. Temporality temporalizes itself as a future which makes present in the process of having been."[11] Another way of putting this is to say that Dasein as past, present, and future is not merely a series of disconnected nows but a unity of these temporal dimensions.

Dasein as temporal, then, is a unity of past, present, and future. But in the authentic mode of existing, Heidegger argues that it is the future which has priority. As ahead of itself, Dasein lives resolutely in the face of its own possibilities. It does not flee this responsibility for its being by retreat into the past or absorption into the present. This future includes one's Being-towards-death, and hence an awareness of one's limit or finiteness. In referring to death in this case, Heidegger is not pointing merely to an end to a series of nows. Rather, it is in Being-towards-death that Dasein is said to be grasped as a whole. Death marks an end, a boundary to the possibilities of existence. It is one's "ownmost" possibility and if not avoided or covered up opens up to responsibility for one's own way of being.

Death is only one of the ends or boundaries by which the totality of Dasein is said to be disclosed. At the other end is the beginning, the birth. "Only that entity which is 'between' birth and death presents the whole," the unity of Dasein.[12] Again we must be careful not to limit our understanding to the ordinary conception of time. Birth is not just the beginning of a series of nows, and the unity of Dasein cannot be merely the series of nows between birth and death. This would be to seek the connectedness or unity of

Dasein from outside Dasein and to treat it as a mere thing. From Dasein itself birth is not merely something in the past and death merely something in the future. "Factical Dasein exists as born; and, as born, it is already dying, in the sense of Being-towards-death."[13] It is in this process of stretching along between birth and death, of appropriating into his own way of being in the present both the "ahead" and the "already" that the unity of the temporality of Dasein and authentic selfhood may be attained.

Although much of Heidegger's emphasis is on Dasein's resolute projection of its own Being-in-the-world, it is important to keep in mind that for Heidegger Dasein is always *mit-Dasein*. This is brought into focus when Heidegger refers to the stretching along of Dasein as the historicizing of Dasein and makes it clear that in this we are bound up with other persons. Although authentic existence is primarily futural, it is not independent of one's thrownness and in this thrownness lies one's heritage, one's handing down of possibilities that have come to one.

> The resoluteness in which Dasein comes back to itself, discloses current factical possibilities of authentic existing, and discloses then *in terms of the heritage* which that resoluteness, as thrown, *takes* over...The more authentically Dasein resolves—and this means that in anticipating death it understands itself unambiguously in terms of its ownmost distinctive possibility—the more unequivocally does it choose and find the possibility of its existence, and the less does it do so by accident...Once one has grasped the finitude of one's existence, it snatches one back from the endless multiplicity of possibilities which offer themselves as closest to one—those of comfortableness, shirking, and taking things lightly—and brings Dasein into the simplicity of its fate (*schicksals*). This is how we designate Dasein's primordial historicizing, which lies in authentic resoluteness and in which Dasein *hands* itself *down* to itself, free for death, in a possibility which it has inherited and yet has chosen.[14]

Heidegger is not arguing that our inheritance dictates our future. Rather, it is as resolute, as projecting into the future that we come back to our heritage in relation to which we may understand the possibilities of existing which are open to us. My decisions into the future are not mere accidents or random choices from an endless multiplicity of choices, but choices made within the context of what my heritage brings to me regarding the understanding of human existence. If, however, Dasein is *mit-Dasein,* if it exists essentially in Being-with-others, then its historicizing is also a co-historicizing. In this sense Heidegger understands the temporality of every Dasein to be connected with the historicizing of the community. "Dasein's fateful destiny in and with its 'generation' goes to make up the full authentic historicizing of Dasein."[15] Again we must remind ourselves that this does not mean that past possibilities simply determine the future. The importance of our heritage is not in the past or the present but in the future. History has to do with the possible. History provides us with the recurrence of the possible, but this will take place only if Dasein is open to it, takes it over in resolute repetition, making present this possibility in our own existing into the future.

Authentic existence does not understand itself as just running along in a continual sequence of pure "nows." It is essentially futural and yet as futural brings with it a heritage, a having been which it shares with its community and which may be retrieved in terms of the possibilities of our future. Human activity in this sense may be likened as Charles Sherover suggests "to the activity of a shallow brook, not one which flows straight and direct but one which eddies, gurgles, and curls back on itself around rocks and stones while it is continually wending its way downstream."[16]

Thus far I have suggested that much of our Western talk of God has been modelled on our talk of persons. The dualistic and static model of persons has resulted in an understanding of God as separated from the world, timeless and irrelevant to a world of growth and change. I have also suggested that more recent studies of the meaning of human existence have emphasized the uniqueness of persons among entities in the world, and I have sought in particular to elucidate Heidegger's understanding of the human experience of time or the temporality of human existence. In the remaining portion of this paper I want to take up Heidegger's suggestion that God's eternity be understood as a more primordial and infinite temporality. Although Heidegger has not himself followed through on this suggestion it is clear that if God is construed on the model of infinite temporality, the result will be a more dynamic understanding of God and a more intimate relationship between God and the world.

In following up on Heidegger's suggestion, it is important that we keep in mind that while Heidegger is suggesting an analogy between the being of God and the being of persons, he is not suggesting an identity or that there is no sense in which we can speak of the transcendence of God to man and the world. Heidegger suggests not that we speak of the temporality of God but that we speak of God's infinite temporality. The distinction between man's finite temporality (*endliche Zeitlichkeit*) and God's infinite temporality (*unendliche Zeitlichkeit*) makes this clear. This suggests not that God is other than temporal but that God is more than temporal, that his temporality in some sense transcends and presumably includes within itself the temporality of finite persons.

If God is construed as infinite temporality, the unity or subsistence of God would not consist in his substantiality in the sense of being essentially complete within himself. Temporality suggests becoming, being in process, or realization. We may in some sense talk of inanimate objects as complete, but such talk is misleading when it comes to persons and by analogy to God. The essence of a person for Heidegger lies in his existence, in his standing out or projecting himself into the future. Indeed, when a person ceases to grow, ceases to project his possibilities, we tend to think of him as less than a person in the fullest sense. We might say such a person has stagnated, has become a mere thing. To talk of a person as becoming is not of course to rule out talk of his being. It is being which becomes. Being and becoming must be related in some way so as to form one reality. As John Macquarrie puts it, "Whatever becomes, must, in some sense, *already be;* yet the fact that it is becoming implies that it *is not yet* what it is on the way to becoming."[17]

Traditionally, some theists have resisted talking of God in this manner and as a result they have had difficulty speaking of God as acting, as responding to developments within the history of the world. God has been held to be immutable, unchanging where change has been understood to suggest a lack of perfection. Yet in our talk of persons, change or becoming does not suggest a defect or lack of perfection. On the contrary, becoming seems essential to perfection. A static or unchanging person would be one who has fallen away from his potentialities, one who is less than a person.

Becoming and change are defects in persons only where there is a lack of vision, a lack of direction, a falling away from a steadfastness of character. Presumably, the phrase "steadfastness of character" would also be applicable to God, but this suggests only that God's becoming must be in accordance with his character, not that he is in every sense unchanging.

Talk of God as infinite temporality would also call into question traditional theistic talk of the timelessness of God. Heidegger suggests correctly, I believe, that talk of the timelessness of God is rooted in the ordinary conception of time in which time is understood as a series of "nows." To say that God is in time in this sense would seem to suggest that God is in some sense bound to this series of "nows," swept along from moment to moment as if time were more ultimate than God. But on the model of temporality neither man nor God is in time in the sense of being bound by it. Human existence is not merely in time but within the limits of birth and death, and takes time into itself in its unification of its anticipated future and remembered past. By analogy God as infinite temporality would not be bound by time and thus need not be conceived as timeless in order to avoid making God dependent on something outside God. As infinite temporality, God would be construed as taking all possibilities of being into itself, of unifying in himself all anticipated futures and remembered pasts. This is not to say, of course, that God has a beginning and an end as if to say that beginning and end are outside of God. Rather, all beginnings and endings must in some sense be within God.

According to Heidegger human existence as temporal stretches itself along and is stretched along, and this is called the historicizing of Dasein. It is not so much that Dasein is in history as that it exists historically. And insofar as Dasein exists essentially with others, its historicizing is said to be a co-historicizing, a sharing with others a common destiny. Putting this in other terms, we might say that Dasein as temporal is relational and that being related is essential to being personal. Now presumably one would not speak of God as being stretched along. But there does seem to be a sense in which one would want to say that God stretches along and in this connection one might speak of God's historicity. This is not to say that God is subsumed in history because history would then be in some sense outside of God and greater than God. It would be, however, to reject an understanding of God as supra-historical, outside of history. Although the Scottish theologian Ronald Gregor Smith differs in many ways from Heidegger, he was perhaps getting at a similar point when he suggested that to speak of God as historical is not to include God within history, like a spirit in a bottle or a ghost in a machine, but to include history in God.[18]

To speak of the historicity of God in the context of talk of God's infinite temporality is not to deny transcendence to God or to reduce God to the story of man's co-historicizing. It is to say in some sense that the destiny of the historicizing of Dasein with others is ultimately the destiny of God, that it is through this historicizing that God comes to self-realization and expression. The end of this historicizing, to use the language of Macquarrie, "would be all things gathered up into God, at one among themselves and at one with Being from which they have come and for which they are destined. But this end too could not be thought of as a point that will eventually be reached, for at every point new vistas will open up."[19]

NOTES

1 C. J. Webb, *God and Personality* (London: George Allen and Unwin, 1918), 61-88.

2 Paul Tillich, *Systematic Theology* (Chicago: University of Chicago Press, 1951), 1:244.

3 Martin Heidegger, *Being and Time,* trans. John Macquarrie and Edward Robinson (New York: Harper & Row, 1962), 67.

4 Richard Swinburne, *The Coherence of Theism* (Oxford: Clarendon, 1977), 210-27.

5 Heidegger, *Being and Time,* 499 n. xiii.

6 Schubert Ogden, "The Temporality of God," in *The Reality of God* (New York: Harper & Row, 1963); Charles Sherover, "Experiential Time and the Religious Concern," *Zygon* 16, no. 4 (December 1981); John Macquarrie, *Principles of Christian Theology,* 2d ed. (New York: Scribner's, 1977). I have discussed Macquarrie's idea of God in "John Macquarrie on God," *Perspectives in Religious Studies* 7, no. 3 (Fall 1980).

7 Heidegger, *Being and Time,* 473-74.

8 Ibid., 466.

9 Ibid., 478.

10 Ibid., 351.

11 Ibid., 401.

12 Ibid., 425.

13 Ibid., 426.

14 Ibid., 435.

15 Ibid., 436.

16 Sherover, 328.

17 Macquarrie, 111.

18 Ronald Gregor Smith, *The Doctrine of God* (London: Collins, 1970), 167.

19 Macquarrie, 359.

Time and Eternity in Royce and Bergson

Milič Čapek

This essay is reprinted from Revue Internationale De Philosophie,
no. 79-80 (1967) with the permission of the author and the publisher.

To compare Royce's and Bergson's views on the relation of time and eternity is of more than purely historical interest. It is true that they both are now regarded as classical thinkers. Royce died a half century ago, Bergson a quarter century ago. Their treatments of the relation of time and eternity appeared at the threshold of the century—that of Royce in the second volume of *The World and the Individual* in 1901, that of Bergson in his article "L'Introduction à la Métaphysique," published in *Revue de Mètaphysique et de Morale* in 1903, and considerably later incorporated into the book *La Pensée et le Mouvant* (1934). An anticipatory hint of Bergson's view can be found in the last chapter of *Matière et Mémoire* (1896). It is certainly interesting that in many respects the views of both thinkers on this problem are remarkably similar, even though they did not know each other's writings at that time: neither did Royce refer to Bergson nor did Bergson refer to Royce. Only about one decade later did Royce discuss Bergson's view of time—but not Bergson's view of eternity—in his article "The Reality of the Temporal," published in the *International Journal of Ethics* in 1910. The similarity, though by no means the identity of both views is even more surprising if we take into consideration the general character of both philosophies: Royce's monistic idealism and eternism, distinctly akin to that of Bradley and Bosanquet, and Bergson's temporalism with its tendency to dualism or at least to the polarity of the mental and the physical. But far more important than the historical affinities and contrasts is the problem itself with which both thinkers dealt. We shall see that it is the generalized form of the problem of the specious present. This problem, called also "the paradox of the simultaneity of succession," still attracts the attention and resists the analytical acumen of contemporary philosophers and psychologists.

Royce and Bergson on Time

Although differently expressed, Royce's and Bergson's analysis of the direct awareness of time are remarkably similar. Like Bergson, Royce not only distinguishes between the perceptual and conceptual knowledge of time, but he also stresses "the highly artificial aspects of our conception of time."[1] On this point Royce's agreement with Bergson became quite explicit in the article referred to above. At that time he was already acquainted with Bergson's distinction between "le temps-durée" and "le temps-longueur"; the first corresponds to the direct perceptual awareness of time, the latter to its symbolical representation. Like Bergson, James, and even Russell, Royce rejects the fiction of infinitely divisible time; but unlike Bergson, Royce—for the reasons which we shall understand later—does not relate the artificial aspects of conceptualized time to the fallacy of spatialization, that is, to the inherent tendency of human intellect to represent the temporal relations by the relations of juxtaposition. We shall see that this is the basic difference which persists under the important similarities between these two systems of thought. We shall deal with the similarities first.

Our experience of time has, according to Royce, two aspects which no adequate interpretation of this experience should disregard: that of *diversity* whose specific temporal form is *succession;* and that of *unity* whose specific temporal form is *duration.* In other words, we perceive the enduring unity of any process, of any change, in spite of the irreversible plurality of its successive phases which are nevertheless perceived as well. But let Royce himself speak:

134

When we more directly experience succession—as, for instance, when we listen to a musical phrase or to a rhythmic series of drum-beats—we not only observe that any antecedent member of the series is over and past before the next member comes, but also, and without the least contradiction between these two aspects of our total experience, we observe that this whole succession, with both its former and later members, so far as with relative directness we apprehend the series of drum-beats, or of other simple events, is present *at once* to our consciousness, in precisely the sense in which the unity of our knowing mental life always finds present at once many facts. It is, as I must insist, true that for my consciousness *b* is experienced as following *a,* and also that both *a* and *b* are *together* experienced as in this relation of sequence.[2]

To illustrate it still more concretely, Royce considers the experience which we have in hearing a line of verse such as "The curfew tolls the knell of parting day":

I unquestionably experience the fact that, for me, every earlier word of the line is over and past before the succeeding word or the last word, *day,* comes to be uttered or to be heard. Yet this is unquestionably not my whole consciousness about the succession. For I am certainly *also* aware that the *whole* line of poetry, as a succession of uttered sounds (or, at all events, a considerable portion of the line), is present to me at once, and as this one succession, when I speak the line. For only by virtue of experiencing this wholeness do I observe the rhythm, the music, and the meaning of the line.[3]

This twofold aspect of the direct experience of time was stressed by Bergson in different words whose meaning nevertheless is not different from that of Royce. One of the most central themes of Bergson's thought is his view that consciousness is inseparable from memory or, more specifically, that consciousness is by its own nature "mnemic," being a prolongation of the past into the present. How close this view is to that of Royce will become obvious if we compare the concrete illustrations which both Bergson and Royce use to make their analysis of the temporal consciousness clearer. For all practical purposes their illustrations are identical:

Now consciousness signifies, above everything, memory. At this moment that I am conversing with you, I pronounce the word "conversation." Clearly, my consciousness presents the word all at once, otherwise it would not be a whole word, and would not convey a single meaning. Yet, when I pronounce the last syllable of the word, the three first have already been pronounced; they are past with regard to the last one, which must then be called the present. But I did not pronounce this last syllable "tion" instantaneously. The time, however short, which I uttered it is decomposable into parts, and all of these parts are past in relation to the last one. This last would be the definite present, were it not, in its turn, decomposable. So that, however you try, *you cannot draw a line between the past and the present, nor consequently, between memory and consciousness...* As a matter of fact, when I pronounce the word "conversation," there is present in my mind not only the beginning, the middle and the end of the word, but also the words which preceded it and all the beginning of the sentence; otherwise I should have lost the thread of my speech.[4] (Italics mine)

In other words, both Royce and Bergson agree that consciousness is never instantaneous in the mathematical sense of the word "instant," but that it is always coexistence with a certain interval of duration. William James pointed out the artificial and fictitious character of the mathematical "knife-edge present" prior to both Bergson and Royce in his *Principles of Psychology;* but he is fair enough to recognize that this was pointed out before him by E. R. Clay—who coined the term "specious present"—and by S. H. Hodgson. However, both Hodgson and Clay still believed that the real present is strictly instantaneous; the enduring psychological present is merely apparent, "specious"—the very choice of the term "specious present" by Clay betrays his underlying belief that the true objective time is a dense continuum of strictly dimensionless instants, each of which "lasts" for an infinitely short time, perishing in the same act in which it is born. This structure of the objective time is hidden to us by our hazy, "specious" psychological present.[5] This belief, to which even James in his first period as well as the young Whitehead adhered, persists even today; it is logically implied in the view that regards the physical reality—and consequently also the physical time—as the primary and objective reality of which our consciousness—including the temporal consciousness—is a mere fragmentary, unreliable, "subjective" and confused echo. The attitude of both Bergson and Royce is significantly different. They both regard the conscious datum as *epistemologically prior* to the conceptual construction; more specifically, the temporal datum, epistemologically prior to the public construct of physical time, offers us a more reliable clue to the nature of real time. For this reason Clay's terminology should be reversed: it is the enduring psychological present which is real—and it is the durationless mathematical "knife-edge" present which is "specious."

What both Royce and Bergson equally insist upon is that in the direct experience of time no clear-cut distinction can be drawn between the present and the past, between succession and duration or between the present pulse of consciousness and its immediate memory. This is what Royce calls the "twofold aspect" of the temporal experience—and any view which fails to take into account both aspects, misrepresents, according to Royce, this experience. This is certainly true of those who claim that *on the logical grounds* no experience of succession is possible:

Sometimes, for the sake of a laudable attempt to define the term *present* in a wholly unambiguous way, those who are giving an account of our experience of time are led to assert that, since every part or element of any series of temporal events can be *present* only when all the other elements of the series are temporally non-existent, i.e. are either past or future, it must therefore be quite impossible for us to be conscious, *at once*, of a present succession involving a series of such elements...To comprehend how I can become in any sense aware of the series of successive words that constitutes the line of verse, such students of our problem are accustomed to say that when any one word as *passing*, or *day*, is present to my mind, the other words, even of the same line, can be present to consciousness *only* as coexistent memories or images of the former words, or as images of the expected coming words. From this point of view, I never really observe any sequence of conscious events as a sequence at all. I merely apprehend each element by itself; and I directly conclude from the images which in my experience are coexistent with this element, that there have been antecedent, and will be subsequent events in the series.[6]

Within such a view, Royce correctly observes, no experience of succession is possible at all. There would be no possibility to differentiate between our experience of time sequence and our experience of juxtaposition. A melody in which the tones succeed each other would be indistinguishable from the chord in which the same tones are simultaneous; the visual perception of the motion—for instance of the shooting star—would be indistinguishable from the luminous trail which it leaves behind it on the sky, and which consists of the juxtaposed luminous points. This is the famous *theory of temporal signs* which tries to explain the perception—or rather the illusion—of succession by the superposition of the cerebral processes of unequal intensity; while the fading cerebral processes corresponding to the past sensations are still going on, the present one reaches its maximum intensity. These differences of unequal intensity of the simultaneously occurring cerebral processes is "translated" by the mind into the differences of their temporal order. That this explanation of the experienced immanence of the past in the present is hardly satisfactory was keenly felt by Theodore Lipps himself, one of those who upheld the theory of "temporal signs"; he frankly conceded that the mind's translation of the order of intensity into the temporal order is entirely inexplicable.[7] Moreover, as Bergson pointed out, the successive states of the brain, strictly speaking cannot overlap in time, being temporally as sharply separated as the successive stages of *any* material system.[8] The physiological fact that several processes of unequal intensity go on simultaneously is something *entirely different* from the psychological merging of the past into the present. On one side we have the physical present which is practically (even if, according to the most recent views, not absolutely) an infinitely thin boundary between past and future; on the other side, the sensible present with a certain temporal breadth.

The theory of temporal signs which reduces the perception of succession to the coexistence of unequally intense sensations or images, has still another difficulty which both Bergson and Royce pointed out. If, in keeping the difference between the present and the past as sharp as possible, we confine the awareness of succession into a single present moment, the question arises: How long is this present moment? Or in Royce's words:

In vain do you suppose that, at any time, you have directly present to your consciousness only one of the successive words that you hear me speak. Not thus do you escape our difficulty. For a spoken word is itself a series of temporally successive sounds. Can you hear at once the whole spoken word, or can you grasp at once this whole series? If so, my foregoing account is in principle admitted.[9]

This passage is strongly reminiscent of that quoted above in which Bergson pointed out that even one word consists of successive sounds and that in its auditory perception the past merges with the present. In truth, as soon as we concede the non-existence of the mathematical present, the immanence of the past in the present is conceded; for the enduring present, being a temporal interval, is, to use Bergson words, "a condensation of the past" in which the present is merged with the immediate memory. Then only two consistent alternative views are open to us: either to claim that the only genuine present—even in the introspective realm—is the knife-edge mathematical instant, and what we call "psychological present" is merely a "loose" or "specious" one; or we must deny the durationless present altogether and admit that the present and the past are *not* externally related and that no phase of the past, no anterior event, no matter how remote in time is *completely* external to the present moment. Such an alternative was clearly formulated by C. A. Strong in his polemic against James's notion of the enduring present; he concluded that since the only true present is strictly instantaneous, that is, completely devoid of duration, "immediate memory" is nothing but an illusion:

To take this illusion seriously is to be guilty of a sort of naive realism in the field of time. The impossibility of such a direct consciousness of time appears, further, from the consequences to which it should lead if true. If we can be directly conscious of a feeling that occurred a half second ago, in spite of the fact that the feeling is past and gone, why not also of a feeling that occurred a whole second ago or a minute ago, or an hour or a day or a week? The consciousness would be in no wise more miraculous. Why cannot we be directly conscious of any past experience, no matter how remote? If such consciousness is not to be thought of, then for the same reason the direct consciousness of a half second ago is not to be thought of ... [10]

139

In other words, we do not perceive the passage of time for, as Strong claims, "the lapse of time is never directly experienced, but constructed after the event." On this point the views of both Bergson and Royce are diametrically opposed to that of Strong. They agree with him that the difference between the immediate and mediate memory (or "recall") is only that of degree; but instead of denying the reality of immediate memory, they both accept it as the datum of experience and they find in it the clue to the problem of memory in general. In the passage quoted above Bergson, after stressing the temporal unity not only of a single word, of a sentence and even of the whole antecedent context expressed in the previous sentences, continues:

> Push the argument to its limit, suppose that my speech had been lasting for years, since the first awakening of my consciousness, that it had been carried on in one single sentence, and that my consciousness were sufficiently detached from the future, disinterested enough in action, to be able to employ itself entirely in embracing the total meaning of the sentence: then I should no more seek the explanation of the integral preservation of this entire past than I seek the explanation of the preservation of the three first syllables of "conversation" when I pronounce the last syllable. Well, I believe that our whole psychical existence is something just like this single sentence, continued since the first awakening of consciousness, interspersed with commas, but never broken by full stops. And consequently I believe that our whole past still exists. It exists subconsciously, by which I mean that it is present to consciousness in such a manner that, to have the revelation of it, consciousness has no need to go out of itself or seek for foreign assistance...[11]

The passage just quoted is related to one of the most important and crucial ideas of Bergson's philosophy; it is surprising how little this idea is stressed in various expositions of Bergson's thought. It is his belief that what we call "specious present" is variable in its extent. This fact is well known in psychology; William James as early as 1890 pointed out that the volume of the specious present or what is also called "the span of immediate memory" varies between the maximum of twelve seconds and the minimum of 1/500 sec.[12] In the state of passivity this span is greatly reduced; in the hypnagogic states and during dreams it is reduced to such extent that the immediately preceding moment is at once forgotten; in this way it becomes understandable why various absurdities occurring in the dream, as for instance a change in location, the sudden appearance of a new person, or an equally sudden transformation of a person with whom we converse—briefly, various illogical discontinuities of the dream—are not perceived by the subject when he dreams, but only when he is awake, that is, when the normal temporal span of his consciousness is restored. Thus the difference between the mental state of the person who forgets his premises when he arrives at a fallacious conclusion differs only in degree from the state of the dreamer who does not remember that a second ago he was in a different surrounding and doing different things. At the same time the reduction of the temporal span accounts for the fact that the subjective length of the dream is much longer than the corresponding interval of public time; or that time in the states of intellectual passivity seems to flow considerably more slowly than in the state of intellectual concentration. In other words, there are, as Bergson says, *different degrees of tension* in different durations which determine different degrees of "condensation of the past" in the present, that is, different spans of immediate memory. In his second book Bergson refers to the frequently mentioned cases of "the panoramic vision of the past," occurring at the moments of great physical danger; then the whole personal past is seen in a single, retrospective flash.[13]

But Bergson did not restrict the application of his theory of different "tensions" of duration to psychology. He took the observed variability of the temporal span in psychology as the basis for an extremely original and bold generalization by which he approached the traditional mind-body problem in a completely different and fresh way. According to him, the relation of the physical and the mental should be conceived in the terms of the difference of different tensions of duration. In the physical world, the temporal span is of minimum duration and, in comparison with the normal span of human psychological duration, it may be regarded for practical purposes as equivalent to a single mathematical instant. Bergson, however, insists that this is only approximately true "for every duration is thick; real time has no instants."[14] In insisting that the constitutive events of the material world have a duration which is *almost* vanishing, but never equivalent to the durationless instants of classical physics, especially those which found their expression in the theory of "chronon," that is, of the elementary interval of time which would not be further divisible. All degrees of temporal span are theoretically conceivable between the nearly-zero duration of the physical events and the human psychological duration. It is probable that in this way the peculiarities of the subhuman consciousness may be accounted for. There is hardly any question that the psychological temporal span of even the most intelligent animal does not attain the human span; while it is equally certain that the consciousness even in the lowest animal species is far above the nearly infinitesimal "consciousness" of matter. The roots of Bergson's idea of matter as "mind devoid of memory" may be traced to Leibniz to whom Bergson explicitly refers: *Omne enim corpus est mens momentanea sive carens recordatione, quia conatum simul suum et alienum contrarium... non retinet ultra momentum: ergo caret memoria, caret sensu actionum passionumque suarum, caret cogitatione.* And the very same idea can be found in one of the last essays of Whitehead.[15]

> When memory and anticipation are completely absent, there is complete conformity to the average influence of the immediate past. There is no conscious confrontation of memory with possibility. Such situation produces the activity of mere matter... Thus the universe is material in proportion to the restriction of memory and anticipation.[16]

But we have seen that the psychological present can vary in either direction. The span of immediate memory can either decrease or increase; in the latter case there will be a more "concentrated" duration integrating within itself a large number of successive events. Both Bergson and Royce agree that in increasing the span of immediate memory we move in the direction in which eternity, being a concentration of all duration, lies. But in analyzing more closely the views of both thinkers, we shall see also important differences between them.

Royce's View of Eternity

The twofold aspect of temporal experience, or, more specifically, the perception of succession, is used by Royce as a model for understanding at least approximately the nature of the divine eternal insight to which the whole temporal order of the world is present at once. "Listen to any musical phrase or rhythm, and grasp it as a whole, and you thereupon have present in you the image, so to speak, of the divine knowledge of the temporal order."[17] Royce strongly insists that his view of eternity does not abolish the temporal order; it merely *includes* it within the unlimited temporal span of Eternal Mind. Remove the rearward and frontward limit of the human specious present; in other words, include the whole past and the whole future within the enormously expanded span of immediate memory, and you will obtain a true image of eternity in which the whole cosmic sequence is included without being abolished. Royce is aware of serious objections which may be raised against it:

> "But," so many hereupon object—"it appears impossible to see how this sort of eternal insight is possible, since just now, in time, the infinite past—including, say, the geological periods and the Persian invasion of Greece, is no *longer,* while the future is *not yet.* How then for God shall this difference of past and future be transcended, and all be seen at once?" I reply, In precisely the same sense all the notes of the melody except this note are *when* this note sounds, but are either *no longer* or *not yet.* Yet you may know a series of these notes at once. Now precisely so God knows the whole time-sequence of the world at once. The difference is merely one of span. You now exemplify the eternal type of knowledge, even as you listen to any briefest sequence of my words. For you, too, know time even by sharing the image of the Eternal.[18]

Thus Royce in an extremely interesting and fresh way reinterprets the famous words of Plato according to which "time is a moving image of eternity." Yet, the question still remains to what extent his image of time is still "moving"; in other words, whether it remains time at all. In what sense does Royce's *totum simul* differ from the timeless omniscient Mind of Laplace? Does not the inclusion of *all* successive phases of the cosmic history into an "Eternal Insight" make them simultaneous, thus abolishing their succession? We already know Royce's answer: no more than our perception of melody makes the successive tones simultaneous; our mind in perceiving a melody does not abolish the succession of its tones; nor does the divine mind abolish the succession of the cosmic events in perceiving them at once. Royce is undoubtedly right when he insists that "at once" for him does not mean *instantaneously at once*. Royce's "at once" (or rather "at once" of Royce's God) is *temporally extended*. This is undoubtedly the most interesting part of Royce's philosophy which sets him definitely apart from other idealists who insist on the timelessness of the Absolute. Anybody who seriously studies this aspect of Royce's philosophy experiences the fascination which his solution exerts, and is greatly tempted to accept it. Did then Royce solve the old vexing problem of co-existence of eternity and succession by using imaginatively the perception of melody as a model for understanding it?

Yet, Royce's model fails in one very important aspect. In our perception of succession, whether it is the succession of tones, of drum-beats, of words, or of successive positions of moving bodies, there is always the awareness of the future which is *beyond* the present, of something *more* to come, of something *not yet* present, yet being on the verge of actualization. Royce is perfectly aware of this characteristic feature of temporal awareness; in truth, it is this feature which leads him to believe that "time is the form of will." Royce correctly related this aspect of temporal awareness to our consciousness of *the direction of time:*

> And this direction of the flow of time can only be expressed in its true necessity by saying that in case of the world's time, as in the case of the time of our inner experience, we conceive the past as leading towards, as aiming in the direction of the future, in such wise that the future depends for its meaning upon the past, and the past in its turn has its meaning as a process expectant of the future. In brief, only in terms of Will, and only by virtue of the significant relations of the stages of a teleological process, has time, whether in our inner experience, or in the conceived world as a whole, any meaning.[19]

Yet, precisely this feature of incompleteness, of a not-yet-realized future transcending the present, is absent in the Roycean Eternity. For the Eternal of Royce is a *completed infinite whole* in which there is no "not yet," no "temporal beyond"; the future—to wit, the whole infinite future—is a part of *totum simul,* of the eternal "At once." But can then Royce still meaningfully claim that time is not abolished? Is it true that his eternal *totum simul* is *temporally* extended? This is extremely doubtful. Let us only recall that only a few lines before the passage quoted Royce explicitly says that *"the direction of the flow of time is a character essential to the very conception of time."* And since the direction of time is linked by Royce—as he explicitly says in the quoted passage—to the *virtuality* of the future to which the past and the present moments point, and since in the divine *At once* the future is actually included and, consequently, is not virtual any longer, it *loses its character of genuine futurity.* Then, according to the very words of Royce, with the elimination of the future *the direction of time disappears as well, and with it time itself.* Such implication is most unwelcome to Royce who did his best to avoid it; but he succeeded only in juxtaposing two incompatible affirmations— one asserting the *totum simul* in which everything is present, the other asserting with an equal emphasis the reality of the temporal order:

> Now the events of the temporal order … are divided, with reference to the point of view of any finite self, into what *now* is, and what *no longer* is, and what *is to be,* but is *not yet.* These same events however, in so far as they are viewed at once by the Absolute, are for such view, all equally present. And this their presence is the presence of all time, as a *totum simul,* to the Absolute. And the presence in this sense, of all time at once to the Absolute, constitutes the Eternal order of the world—eternal, since it is inclusive of all distinctions of temporal past and temporal future—eternal, since for this very reason, the totality of temporal events thus present at once to the Absolute has not events that precede, or that follow it, but contains all sequences within it—eternal, finally, because this view of the world does not, like our partial glimpses of this or that relative whole of sequence, pass away and give place to some other view, but includes an observation of every passing away, of every sequence, of every event and of whatever in time succeeds and follows that event, and includes all the views that are taken by the various finite Selves.[20]

Here Royce admits quite explicitly that the eternal order, while it includes every passing away, *does not itself pass away*. In Royce's God, there is no place for becoming, nor place for "divine self-creation" in the Bergsonian or Hartshornian sense. The totality of time, that is a time wholly elapsed, is no time at all, since the unidirectional irreversible *elapsing* is the very essence of time. Why then does Royce still insist that time is not abolished, but only included in the eternal order? Because, he says, the whole cosmic temporal sequence, that is, all the events with all their temporal characteristics are preserved in the all-embracing Eternal Now. But here Royce fails to see the implications of his own view. In the first place, the event elapsed is by the act of passing away deprived of the specific temporal relations by spatial symbols. For the original event in its process of passing was embedded between its own irrevocable past and the virtualities of its own future. Once passed, what was its own immediate future was transformed into a new present and thus ceased to be virtual; its "not-yet" character is irrevocably lost. But we have to bear in mind that this "not-yet" character of the immediately subsequent event enters into the very constitution of any temporal event; it constitutes its own "temporal specificity." To ignore it is possible only if we regard the temporal events as *mutually external* atomic entities, committing thus what Whitehead called "the fallacy of simple location"—to wit, "simple location in time." Such fallacy is inherent in the language of those who believe that the temporal characteristics of events are exhaustively characterized by assigning to the events different "positions" in the temporal series. Here we see immediately the unfortunate consequences of the persistent habit to symbolize the temporal relations by spatial symbols. For in the language referred to above succession is assimilated to a geometrical line and the events are symbolized by the juxtaposed points or segments on this line. Thus the incomplete character of time is obscured since on the geometrical line the points left of any given point are as actually existing as those lying right of it; succession is thus converted into juxtaposition. Not only this: the geometrical items—whether the points or segments—symbolizing the events are themselves discrete —thus suggesting erroneously the atomistic character of temporal events. We sink thus into the fallacy of simple location which artificially isolates each event from its temporal context—its ancestors, constituting its past and its not yet existing virtualities, constituting its future.

Royce was aware that the relation of succession is different from that of juxtaposition; let us only recall his refusal to believe that the perception of melody consists of the sensation of one single tone *together with the coexisting memory-images of the antecedent tones.* Yet, he compared explicitly the perception of successive events to the perception of different parts of a single geometrical surface.[21] It is clear that his mind, while resisting the temptation to spatialize time, eventually yielded to it; and this explains why he insisted on the *discreteness* of the temporal series.[22] The atomistic view of the temporal event enabled him then to disregard its temporal context, including the virtualities of its own future. These virtualities are *ex definitione* absent in the Absolute since in the eternal *totum simul* no futurities, no potentialities exist. Thus, ultimately, the succession of events is converted by Royce into the juxtaposed elements of the Infinite Set to which Royce gives the name "Absolute" or "God."

Bergson's View of Eternity

In one place, and in one place only, did Bergson explicitly formulate his view of eternity. Undoubtedly, the *words* "eternal" and "eternity" occur in several places in his writings, but his *idea* of eternity, organically related to the rest of his philosophy, is fully explained only in the following passage of his essay *L'Introduction à la Métaphysique:*

> Strictly speaking, there might exist no other duration than our own, as there might be no other color in the world than orange, for example. But just as a consciousness of color, which would harmonize inwardly with orange instead of perceiving it outwardly, would feel itself caught between red and yellow, would perhaps even have, beneath the latter color, a presentiment of a whole spectrum in which is naturally prolonged the continuity which goes from red to yellow, so the intuition of our duration, far from leaving us suspended in the void as pure analysis would do, puts us in contact with a whole continuity of durations which we should try to follow either downwardly or upwardly: in both cases we can dilate ourselves indefinitely by a more and more vigorous effort, in both cases transcend ourselves. In the

first case, we advance toward a duration more and more scattered, whose palpitations, more rapid than ours, dividing our simple sensation, dilute its quality: at the limit would be the pure homogeneous, the pure *repetition* by which we shall define materiality. In advancing in the other direction, we go toward a duration which stretches, tightens, and becomes more and more intensified: at the limit would be eternity. This time not only conceptual eternity, which is an eternity of death, but an eternity of life. It would be a living and consequently still moving eternity where our own duration would find itself like the vibrations in light, and which would be the concretion of all duration as materiality is its dispersion. Between these two extreme limits moves intuition, and this movement is metaphysics itself.[23]

A briefer, but a similar passage appeared about eight years later, in his Oxford lecture "La perception du changement":

In fact, the more we accustom ourselves to think and to perceive all things *sub specie durationis,* the more we plunge into real duration. And the more we immerse ourselves in it, the more we set ourselves back in the direction of the principle, though it be transcendent, in which we participate and whose eternity is not to be an eternity of immutability, but an eternity of life: how, otherwise, could we live and move in it? *In ea vivimus et movemur et sumus.*[24]

Like Royce, Bergson in his meditation about eternity starts from a very concrete experience—that of the temporal span of our present moment. Like Royce, Bergson is aware that the boundaries of the psychological present are dim and shifting; in other words, that the temporal span varies. But while Royce states this fact abstractly, Bergson in *Matière et Mémoire* and in several essays of *L'Energie spirituelle* illustrates it by a number of concrete examples which would be too long here to enumerate. For our purpose suffice it to say that there is hardly a more important idea of Bergson's psychology, and of his metaphysics than that of what he calls "la tension de la durée" or "la concentration du passé dans le présent." Different degrees of "durational tension," that is, of different span of duration, account, according to Bergson, for the differences between the passive and active attitudes or "levels" of mind. When our psychological duration is more "diluted," that is when the mnemic span of our psychological present is considerably shortened, the rhythm of our stream of consciousness is accelerated in the sense that what is perceived by us in the state of intellectual or volitional concentration as a single quality, disintegrates in the consciousness of the dreamer into the series of quicker successive pulses. We cannot go here into details and to show how Bergson in this way explained certain peculiarities of the dream and of the related phenomena, in particular of "fausse reconnaissance." This is the meaning of Bergson's words that mind, in relaxing its temporal tension "moves in the direction of matter and spatiality."[25] As we mentioned in the first part of this study, he explains in this way the difference between the "mental" and the "physical"; the events of the physical world, though not instantaneous, are incomparably shorter than the constituting events of even the most diluted duration of a psychasthenic or of a dreamer. We have seen how this idea of matter as *mens momentanea* or "perpetual forgetting" can be traced back to the young Leibniz.

On this point there is the first important difference between Bergson (and Leibniz) on one side and Royce on the other side: Royce does not consider any temporal spans shorter than the span of normal human consciousness. Consequently, his philosophy of nature—if we can even speak of it—looks drastically different. In truth, his view of matter is the very opposite to that of Bergson:

> we should at once suppose that the actually fluent inner experience, which our hypothesis attributes to inorganic nature, would be a finite experience of *an extremely august temporal span,* so that a material region of the inorganic world would be to us the phenomenal sign of the presence of at least one fellow-creature who took, perhaps, a billion years to complete a moment of his consciousness...Nature would be thus the sign of the presence of other finite consciousness than our own, whose time-span was in general very different from ours, but whose rationality, whose dignity, whose significance, whose power to will, whose aptness to pursue ideals, might *be equal to or far above our own*...[26] (Italics added)

This is undoubtedly the source of Royce's pantheism, so significantly different from the dualistically oriented philosophy of Bergson: man's mind is for him on the bottom of the temporal scale, and the temporal span of both inorganic nature and God are far "more auguste" than man's. *Deus sive natura* seems to hold for Royce as much as for Spinoza, but certainly not for Bergson.[27]

The second most significant difference then consists in Bergson's explicit emphasis on *"the moving"* character of his eternity. "Conceptualized eternity" (*l'éternité conceptuelle*) is for Bergson "the eternity of death" while the eternity of life is a *living* and, consequently *moving* eternity in which our own duration would be contained in a similar way in which the very short vibrations of the electromagnetic waves are contained within the duration of our visual perception. In other words, the divine duration is related to our psychological duration in the same way in which our psychological duration is related to the duration of the elementary physical events. The material events—we must not forget that for Bergson, like for Whitehead, Bachelard, and Russel matter consists of the events—are on the bottom of the durational scale on the top of which is his "éternité vivante." Hence his metaphysical dualism —or rather metaphysical polarity—which is completely absent in Royce's thought.

But there are ambiguities and difficulties in Bergson's view. In the first place, how can a shorter duration be "contained"—note the spatial connotation of the word "contain"—within a larger one without losing its own durational, incomplete character? How can an enormously large number of successive events be condensed in a single pulse of a larger duration? This is obviously another form of the problem of "the simultaneity of succession" known also under the name "the paradox of specious present." Bergson's answer certainly would be that the co-extensiveness—or rather *co-presence* of several durations of different temporal span is *empirically given,* and if this experience resists our effort of conceptualizing it, so much worse for our conceptualization—*not* for the experience itself! For every second of our perception of red color, for instance, is co-present with four hundred milliards of successive electromagnetic vibrations; similarly, every second of our indivisible sensation of the tone *a* is co-present with 435 vibrations in the air.[28] In a similar way, as Bergson hinted already in *Matière et Mémoire,* the whole of human history can be lived in a few moments by a consciousness of a larger durational span.[29]

Thus this difficulty exists only for those who tend to overlook the fact that the existence of the durations of different rhythms belongs to the facts of our daily experience. Furthermore, we must not forget that Bergson's "living eternity" is still "moving," that is, its forward edge is "bounded" by the unrealized future. In other words, it is *not* Royce's *totum simul* in which *all* the future is actualized; it still moves forward, "futurewards," beyond itself.[30] In Royce's *totum simul* there is no temporal "beyond," no virtualities at all. But if Bergson's eternity is bounded, is it still an eternity? Does it not become finite? Not necessarily. Although limited or—which is the same—*moving* in the direction of future, Bergson's all-embracing duration may be infinite in the direction of the past. The words "concretion of the whole of duration" (*concrétion de toute durée*) would then mean a concretion *of the whole past eternity*. But this interpretation is not true; it would imply that Bergson accepted the actual infinity. Now every evidence points to the conclusion that Bergson was a *finitist,* that is, that he resolutely *rejected* the concept of actual infinity—the same concept which Royce enthusiastically accepted. Not only did Bergson explicitly reject the concept of the *spatially infinite* universe;[31] not only did he accept the finitism of François Evellin whose analysis of Zeno's paradoxes he viewed as "conclusive";[32] but, if we trust the information supplied relatively recently by Jacques Chevalier, he rejected in 1901 *both* spatial and temporal infinity of the world in linking the thesis in Kant's third antinomy to the thesis in the first antinomy:

> If there is the origin of the universe, if its duration is finite, there is freedom at the beginning of everything, and consequently, in the nature of things. If, on the other hand, there is no origin of the universe, if its duration is infinite and eternal, if there is no absolute beginning, there cannot be any freedom within the Causal series.[33]

It is very probable that Bergson was on this point influenced by Renouvier who never tired of stressing the correlation of infinitism and necessitarianism—the correlation which exists in Royce's thought too. Bergson's rejection of necessitarianism then naturally led him *in the direction of finitism,* even though his rejection of the beginningless eternity of the world in *Creative Evolution* was more hesitant and more ambiguous than Chevalier wanted us to believe.[34]

Does it mean then that for Bergson to speak of eternity was a mere *façon de parler?* This is probable—unless we understand his "eternity" in the sense of "open infinity," that is, "open in the direction of the future"—in other words, "potential infinity" in the Aristotelian sense. Nothing agrees more with Bergson's idea of "open future" which led him to reject not only mechanism, but radical finalism as well, the latter being labeled by him as "inverted mechanism" ("mécanisme à rebours"). For finalism by insisting that the evolution of the world fulfills in all details the program outlined in advance virtually eliminates novelty as effectively as mechanism, especially when it insists—as Royce does—that on the highest metaphysical level this program is *already realized.* But even a milder form of finalism which, while conceding the reality of novelty and contingency in the cosmic history, still insists that the final goal will be eventually attained, is charged by Bergson with "closing the future" and thus limiting the eternity—to wit, "the open eternity" in the sense explained above.

It is beyond the scope of this essay to explore the similarities and differences between Bergson's "open society" and Royce's "infinite community."[35] Suffice it to say that the similarities are due to the common belief of both thinkers that "time is a form of will." While Royce says it explicitly, Bergson says it usually in different words, but in one place even explicitly, when he calls his *élan vital* "pure willing" (*pur vouloir*)[36] which moves in the direction of the "open society" in a similar sense in which for Royce time, as a form of restless will, moves toward "the infinite community." But, again, the basic difference between both thinkers remains, and it is due to the fact that Royce's temporalism is *not* genuine. If the final goal, the final synthesis is already attained, if the striving itself is suspended and all the evil overcome in the *totum simul,* does not any effort, any struggle become superfluous? Do not evil and tragedy then lose their seriousness? This is an uncomfortable moral—or rather quietistic—consequence which every static or implicitly static view faces; and there is hardly any question that in spite of honest and serious effort "to take time seriously," Royce's thought moved to the conclusion of Bradley and McTaggart: that "ultimately" time is unreal.

NOTES

1 Josiah Royce, *The World and the Individual* (London: Macmillan, 1901), 2:113.

2 Ibid., 2:115.

3 Ibid., 2:116.

4 Henri Bergson, *Mind-Energy* (London: Macmillan, 1920), 68-69.

5 William James, *The Principles of Psychology* (New York: Henry Holt, 1890), 1:608-10.

6 Royce, *The World and the Individual*, 2:118.

7 James, 1:632 n.

8 Henri Bergson, *Matière et Mémoire* (1896), 162.

9 Royce, *The World and the Individual*, 2:120.

10 C. A. Strong, "Consciousness and Time," *The Psychological Review* 3 (1896): 156.

11 Bergson, *Mind-Energy*, 60.

12 James, 1:612-14.

13 For a more detailed discussion of this phenomenon and Bergson's explanation of it, see the article of Georges Poulet, "Bergson et le théme de la vision panoramique du passé," in *Revue de Théologie et de Philosophie* 10 (1960): 21-41.

14 Henri Bergson, *Durée et simultanéité*, 3d ed. (Paris: Alcan, 1926), 68.

15 *Theoria motus abstracti, Phil Werke*, ed. Gerhardt, 4:230.

16 Alfred North Whitehead, *The Interpretations of Science*, ed. A. H. Johnson (Indianapolis: Bobbs-Merrill, 1961), 262.

17 Royce, *The World and the Individual*, 2:145.

18 Ibid.

19 Ibid., 2:132.

20 Cf. Charles Hartshorne, *Man's Vision of God* (Hamden, Conn.: Archon, 1941), chap. 7; also "Whitehead's Idea of God," in *The Philosophy of A. N. Whitehead*, ed. Paul Schilpp (LaSalle, Ill.: Open Court, 1951), 541-46; Royce, *The World and the Individual*, 2:141.

21 Ibid., 2:115.

22 Ibid., 2:138: "Nevertheless, in the last analysis, the Absolute Will must be viewed in a well-ordered and discrete series of facts, which from our point of view may indeed appear, as we shall still further see, capable of discrimination *ad infinitum.*" The last part of this quotation seems to imply that Royce, contrary to his other utterances, believed in the infinite divisibility of even the smallest temporal interval!

23 Henri Bergson, *La Pensée et le Mouvant* (Paris, 1934), 237-38; and *The Creative Mind*, trans. M. L. Andison (New York: Philosophical Library, 1946), 220-21.

24 Bergson, *Pensée*, 199; *The Creative Mind*, 186.

25 Cf. also *Creative Evolution*, trans. Arthur Mitchell (New York: Henry Holt, 1911), 219-22; *L'évolution créatrice*, 62d ed. (Paris: Presses Universitaires de France, 1946), 201-4.

26 Royce, *The World and the Individual*, 2:228.

27 Cf. the quotation above from "La perception du changement" where Bergson stresses the *transcendence* of his eternal principle. This foreshadows Bergson's words in *Les deux sources de la morale et de la religion* (9th ed., 1932) when he speaks of mystics as "distincts de Dieu." Cf. also his rejection of "pantheism and monism in general" in his letter to P. Joseph de Tonquedec, 20 Feb. 1912. Cf. *Henri Bergson, Écrits et Paroles*, ed. R. M. Mossé-Batide (Paris: Presses Universitaires de France, 1959), 2:365-66.

28 This fact is only differently expressed in *Durée et Simultanéité* (p. 68) where Bergson, while rejecting with Einstein "the simultaneity of instants," insists that it is meaningful to speak of *the simultaneity of the intervals* ("la simultanéité des flux"). The co-presence of the indivisible sensory quality with a great number of successive physical events is an instance of "the simultaneity of the fluxes."

29 Bergson, *Matière et Mémoire*, 232.

30 Cf. Professor D. Zwiebel's excellent essay "Durée de Dieu et Imprévisibilité des actes libres chez Bergson" in which he pointed out the impossibility to reconcile Bergson's idea of "living eternity" with the traditional idea of predestination which implies the timelessness of the divine insight. (Bergson et nous, *Actes du Xᵉ Congrès des sociétés de philosophie de langue française, Bulletin de la Société française de Philosophie*, 53d annual, 343-46; 54th annual, 178-82.)

31 Bergson, *L'évolution créatrice*, 245; *Creative Evolution*, 266.

32 Bergson, *L'évolution créatrice*, 311; *Creative Evolution*, 338.

33 Jacques Chevalier, *Entretiens avec Bergson* (Paris: Plon, 1959), 5 (Eng. trans. Milič Čapek).

34 On one place of *Creative Evolution* (p. 262 of English translation, p. 241 of the French original) Bergson apparently rejects both the eternity of matter and its instantaneous creation. Bergson does not indicate what the third possibility could be.

35 About this, see John E. Smith, *Royce's Social Infinite* (New York: Liberal Arts Press, 1950).

36 Bergson, *L'évolution créatrice*, 239; *Creative Evolution*, 260.

God as Alpha and Omega: Dipolar Process Theism

Gene Reeves

P rocess theology is often presented and understood as proposing a conception of God which stands fundamentally
in contrast with traditional views. While this understanding is basically correct if Process theism is compared with a
particular tradition such as classical theism, the thesis of this
paper is that this understanding is false if Process theism is compared
with traditional views as a whole. That is, rather than a simple
repudiation of previous ways of thinking about God, Process theism
can be understood as a way of incorporating a diversity of otherwise
incompatible traditional views within a single coherent conception
of God. Especially, traditional philosophical and religious views
are brought together in a meaningful way. Thus, the originality or
novelty of Process theism lies not in its overcoming of older views
but in its synthesis of diverse traditional views.

The operating principle which makes this synthesis possible is
the dipolar concept of God, a conception which was virtually
stumbled upon and inadequately articulated by Alfred North
Whitehead, and developed extensively by Charles Hartshorne.
This paper makes a very brief presentation of this historical development within Process thought, and then attempts to show the
merits of the Hartshornian synthesis.

Whitehead and Hartshorne

Because Whitehead's various conceptions of God are not necessarily inconsistent, it is not obvious that they developed rather rapidly. In *Science and the Modern World,* God is merely the *principle* of limitation, an abstract principle which in various traditions has been called "Jehovah, Allah, Brahma, Father in Heaven, Order of Heaven, First Cause, Supreme Being, Chance."[1] In *Religion in the Making,* delivered as lectures in the same year that *Science and the Modern World* was published, God is no longer a mere principle but an "actual but nontemporal entity," one of the formative elements which constitute actual occasions.[2] Whitehead's thought about God is most fully presented in *Process and Reality;* but even in most of that book it is the principle of limitation, now developed into the "primordial nature of God," that figures prominently. Only in the final chapter do we find significant discussion of "the consequent nature" of God. The relation between the two natures is not discussed, leading some critics to claim that for all practical purposes Whitehead might have been speaking of two different Gods. Still, however inadequately developed, it is clear that Whitehead held a dipolar view of God, one in which the two poles, primordial and consequent, are analogous to the two poles, conceptual and physical, of ordinary actual occasions.[3]

For designating the two poles of God, Hartshorne has usually preferred the terms "abstract" and "concrete." Some of Hartshorne's statements suggest that his views are identical with Whitehead's.[4] In fact, while they can be reconciled, there are important differences.[5] Perhaps the most important of these differences, and one which is still vigorously debated within Process theism, is that while Whitehead thought of God as a single actual entity, for Hartshorne God is a personally ordered series of occasions, a divine living person. Hartshorne's analogy is not with a single actual occasion, but with a person, conceived as having both an enduring character and a series of concrete actual states which successively embody that character. God has an abstract, eternal, and necessary essence which is contained within an infinite number of temporally ordered concrete states of existence. Accordingly, there are divine functions, such as providing initial aims to creatures, assigned by Whitehead to the primordial nature which for Hartshorne must be attributed to God as a whole.

However such important differences between Whitehead and Hartshorne may be worked out within Process thought, it is primarily Hartshorne's conceptually more rigorous scheme which provides the basis for subsequent discussion in this paper.[6]

Alpha and Omega

One minor problem with Hartshorne's presentations of the divine polarity is the absence of truly appropriate designations for the two poles in general, both of which can reasonably be described in several different ways. Consider the following set of metaphysical polar categories.

abstract and concrete
absolute and relative
being and becoming
necessary and contingent
eternal and temporal
permanent and changing
independent and dependent
active and passive
one and many
unity and diversity
simple and complex (or compound)
cause and effect

While some of these contrasts are very closely related in meaning, perhaps none are strictly equivalent. More important, none of them obviously includes all of the others, and no one adequately names all of the others. So, for purposes of this discussion, I propose to use the designations "Alpha" and "Omega" to refer respectively to those categories to the left and on the right. An assumption is that the terms Alpha and Omega are relatively deficient of meaning, though the suggestion of beginning and end is not unintended.

No claim is made that this set of polarities is complete. Perhaps others, such as potential/actual and infinite/finite, should be added. There appears to be no satisfactory way of specifying a complete set of metaphysical polarities of this kind, but the above list is reasonably adequate for the purposes of this paper.

Neither have we worked out a systematic approach to determining why a pole of one of these contrasts belongs on the Alpha side rather than the Omega side, and not the reverse. Why do "abstract," "independent," and "one" belong together? Or, on the other hand, "becoming," "passive," and "complex"? I suppose that there is a systematic connection of the Alpha categories to each other and of the Omega categories to each other, and that this connection involves a systematic entailment, but this claim is left undeveloped here. There appears to be sufficient intuitive and historic connection between them to serve the purposes of this paper and to name them collectively Alpha and Omega. Accordingly, Alpha designates whatever is supremely abstract, absolute, necessary, eternal, etc., being. Omega refers to whatever is supremely concrete, relative, contingent, etc., becoming.

Monopolar Theism

Within classical thinking about God have been two critical assumptions about such metaphysical contrasts. The first may be termed the "monopolar" assumption. According to it, if an Alpha category can be predicted of any individual, its contrasting Omega category cannot. An individual, it was thought, cannot be both absolute and relative, or both simple and complex, etc. In summary, the assumption was that no individual can be both Alpha and Omega.

The second assumption was that the Alpha categories, or anything described by them, are superior, both ontologically and axiologically, to the Omega categories and what can be described by them. According to this assumption of Alpha superiority, what the Alpha categories describe is both more real and more valuable than what the Omega categories describe.

Both the classical philosophical theism of the West and the philosophical pantheism more characteristically found in India are based on these assumptions. The difference between them is that while theism asserted the superiority of the Alpha categories it also allowed a kind of secondary form of reality and deficient value outside of God for the Omega categories, thus setting up a God and world contrast on the basis of these categories. Pantheism, on the other hand, made the Omega categories merely illusory, completely without reality or significance.

One obvious problem, especially for the pantheistic approach, is whether Alpha categories have any meaning apart from the Omega categories. Is it possible to think a unity apart from some plurality of which the one is a member or integration? Is it possible to think of a cause without effects, or of being which is not a factor in some becoming?

The impossibility of such thinking led quite naturally to the view that no concepts can be applied literally or univocally to God, and to "negative theology." God is neither Alpha nor Omega. In this way, classical theism represents a failure of thought, an example of thought reaching a point where it cannot go without running into logical incoherence. But it is a failure based upon the twin assumptions that the Alpha and Omega categories are mutually exclusive and that the Alpha categories are in all respects superior. And these assumptions continued to work invidiously despite the conclusions about univocal language. On the Alpha side, it was said, there is a transcendent analogue, but not for the Omega side. Thus God is more unitary than one but not more complex than many. It was said that God was beyond all human categories, but it is clear that the Alpha categories and the Omega categories are not the same in this respect.

There are, of course, good and perhaps obvious reasons for doubting the efficacy of human thought to conceptualize anything adequately, and much better and more obvious reasons for affirming the inadequacy of human thought about God. The richness of the depths of lived experience is never captured by concepts. Finite perspectives can never encompass the divine perspective. Fuller human expression—about anything—requires not only careful philosophical analysis but sciences and arts as well. Philosophy is necessarily both very limited and very fallible. But none of this is ground for favoring Alpha categories over Omega ones.

Nor does common human experience provide warrant for this kind of metaphysical favoritism. In everyday life we experience a person as defective who does not integrate his life into some unity, but equally undesirable is a life that is so simple as to be without richness and variety. The good as we experience it is always some unity in variety or variety in unity, some harmony involving both unity and contrast. We struggle against both chaos or pure discord and against monotony and triviality. Similarly, we experience people as defective if they are too exclusively passive, but neither do we want them to be so impassive as to be insensitive, unresponsive, and unadaptable. In every case, what experience tells us is that there are better and worse exemplifications of unity and variety, of activity and passivity, of being and becoming, etc. Accordingly, one might suppose, especially if there is a positive relation between divinity and beauty, that God would be conceived as the supreme excellence and therefore as one who integrates an infinite plurality, and otherwise be describable as both Alpha and Omega.

Similarly, while it might legitimately be claimed that the great historic theistic religious traditions have *favored* a monopolar and Alpha conception of God, it is clearly not the case that such favoritism totally excluded characterizations of God requiring Omega categories. The witness of faith, as expressed in every one of the great historic religious traditions speaks of God being receptive as well as active, influenced as well as creative, temporal as well as eternal—Omega as well as Alpha. One may claim that such language is metaphoric or symbolic or poetic, which of course it is. But it is only by way of some powerful metaphysical assumptions that one can find warrant in religious scriptures and traditions for believing that God is only symbolically responsive love while literally, or at least more literally, eternally immutable, symbolically Omega, and more "really" Alpha.

One should not suppose that the monopolar assumptions attributable to such classical thinkers as Aquinas, Maimonides, Shankara, Asvaghosha and Al-Ghazzali are absent from contemporary theology. In the thought of Paul Tillich, for example, one finds an especially interesting expression of the monopolar problem. Tillich makes much of the three ontological polarities of dynamics and form, individualization and participation, and freedom and destiny. At the level of existence the poles are separated and in conflict with their opposites; at the level of essence they are united but in tension with each other; but at the level of Being-itself—in God—they are united without tension. Thus far we might have the beginnings of a genuinely dipolar conception of God. But Tillich also claims that the polarities are symbols implying a divine ultimacy in which the polarities disappear, suggesting that they do not really apply to God at all.[7] Without any clear conception of how the polar contrasts might be applied to God, that is, how they might be conceived to be united without tension but without disappearing, Tillich is free to express favoritism for one pole over another. Thus, by insisting that Being-itself or God is totally unconditioned, he retains divine freedom but not divine destiny, expressing the traditional Alpha bias. On the other hand, by insisting that God is not a being in any sense, he retains divine participation while losing divine individualization, thus giving expression to an inappropriate Omega bias. Only with respect to dynamics and form, by insisting that God is both Abyss and Logos, is true polarity retained within God.

One obvious reason for the monopolar prejudice is the Platonic view that change implies defect, and therefore that a perfect being cannot possibly be subject to change. But as Hartshorne has effectively argued, "perfection" can be more adequately understood as having no rival, or as being unsurpassable by others while surpassable by self. That is, unlike static perfection, perfection conceived dynamically makes it possible to understand how God would be perfect in knowledge and power and goodness without supposing that everything else is simply deficient in these categories. Accordingly, perfect knowledge or wisdom would consist in knowing clearly and certainly all that can be known, in contrast with unclear, fallible, and enormously limited human knowledge. Such knowledge would be as complete as any knowledge can be, but it would also be a wisdom which is continuously exceeding itself through being enriched by events of the world. Though always incomplete in one sense, such perfect wisdom is in no way defective. Perfect or ultimate power can be understood as power to influence all others and therefore power to insure that from what is given and actual the best possible outcome will ensue. But such ultimate power could not be all power. If it were, the whole interplay between God and the world would be completely pointless; nor would such ultimate power necessarily be sufficient to insure that there will be a good outcome for any one or all of us. Finally, it is the glory of God, or the divine life itself, that is served by divine power. In relation to it our lives stand before divine judgment. Thus, while divine power is necessarily conceived to be limited, it is not defective either in goodness or pervasiveness. In a world in which there is a multiplicity of sometimes incompatible interests, ultimate or perfect goodness consists in adequately taking into account all such interests both actual and possible. A goodness which always seeks the best possible outcome for the whole of reality could not be exceeded even by subsequent states of itself. It too is completely without defect of any kind.

Dipolar Process Theism

If the classical assumptions are that Alpha and Omega cannot be attributed to the same individual and that Alpha is both ontologically and axiologically superior to Omega, process theism can be seen as the reversal of these assumptions. But it is important to recognize that this result is very different from a simple reversal of the classical view, precisely because the rejection of monopolarity makes it impossible to assert a simple conversion of Alpha superiority into Omega superiority.

"Dipolar theism" is the term which most adequately describes process philosophy's rejection of the assumption of monopolarity. As already suggested by rhetorical questions earlier in this paper, our view is not only that there is no good reason for holding that the metaphysical contrasts cannot be attributed to the same individual but that they must be simultaneously attributed to God if either the polar categories or "God" are to be rationally intelligible. According to what Morris Cohen termed the "Principle of Polarity," metaphysical contrasts are correlatives, mutually interdependent on each other for their meaning, so that nothing real can be thought to be describable wholly in Alpha terms or wholly in Omega terms.[8] The abstract can only be an aspect of the concrete and the concrete must be described in terms of abstract aspects, etc. Alpha and Omega require each other, or at least intelligibility requires both.

Accordingly, dipolar theists cannot simply reverse the classical assumption of Alpha superiority by asserting the ontological and axiological superiority of the Omega categories. To claim that being is somehow less real than becoming, or that being is only an illusion of human perspective, would be to violate the principle of polarity as surely as did the classical assumption of Alpha superiority. The result would be merely another kind of unintelligibility.

What process philosophy does claim is that the Omega categories are more inclusive than the Alpha categories. While unchanging being can be a factor, perhaps trivial, perhaps dominant, in a changing whole, the opposite is not the case. While a cause may be, indeed always is, a factor of its effects, the opposite is never the case. While unity must be a factor within any diversity, diversity cannot be included within pure unity. The principle involved here is the relatively simple matter of inclusiveness, basically a matter of logic rather than of ontological or axiological superiority.

Dipolar theism, accordingly, is the view that God is to be conceived as having an Alpha aspect or nature which is included within Omega states. The Alpha categories apply no less than in classical views. God is necessary, absolute being, eternal, independent of all else, purely active cause with simple unity. This is God as mere necessary existence and purely abstract. This essence of God, according to dipolar views, must be understood as an aspect of every concrete or actual state of the divine life. The states of the divine life, however, must be understood in terms of the Omega categories. That is, a concrete state of the divine is a receptive becoming, influenced by everything else and, therefore, relative, dependent, contingent, etc.

Suppose that God were not Omega, that the contingent and relative was entirely outside of God. We would then have a total reality which would be more inclusive than either the world of God, and of which God would be a mere constituent. It makes more sense, both metaphysically and religiously, to conceive of God as the ultimately inclusive—in this sense, transcendent—reality. Of course it would be inappropriate for God to include or know others in the inferior manner in which we include or know others. But inclusiveness in a manner appropriate to deity, that is, in a categorically supreme way unique to deity, is a way of both asserting and understanding divine perfection. For this reason, Hartshorne has sometimes used the term "panentheism" to characterize dipolar Process theism.

Dipolar theism is able to clarify logically how it is that God is both Alpha and Omega, simply by recognizing that there is no law of logic prohibiting attribution of contrasting predicates to the same individual provided they apply to different aspects of that individual.

Does this mean that the contrast between God and the world made possible by the monopolar assumption is lost? Not at all.

For, in dipolar Process theism God is to be understood as categorically superior on both the Alpha and the Omega side. That is, God is the union of categorically supreme independence and categorically supreme dependence, of categorically supreme activity and categorically supreme passivity, of categorically supreme being and categorically supreme becoming. God is not merely more necessary than the creatures (whatever that would mean), God is the only necessary individual. Similarly, God is the only individual who is influenced by, hence relative to, absolutely every other individual. God is supremely one, but also the only one with an infinite number of actual states, thus supremely many. Because God is with all creation, and in this sense before all time, the divine life is uniquely eternal, but, for the same reason, because there is no time when God is not, the divine life is also uniquely temporal. Because God is the one individual on whom all others are dependent, divinity is supremely creator and cause; but, because God is also the only individual who experiences, knows and is influenced by every creature, divinity is the supreme effect or creature of the world. With respect to each of the Alpha and Omega categories, God is as different from every other individual as all from some. In no case is God merely more Alpha or more Omega than others; God alone is both supremely one and supremely many, supremely absolute and relative, etc., that is, categorically Alpha and Omega.

There are, Process theists believe, many advantages to the dipolar conception of God—any one of which would make it preferable to classical nonpolar views. Four or five such advantages will be sketched here.

(1) The dipolar Process view is more rationally coherent. Perhaps it is not obvious to everyone that rational coherence is an advantage. Reason, it can rightly be claimed, distorts experience, and, whenever rationality results in a system of thought which conflicts with experience, we are rightly offended. But surely incoherence is not desirable in itself. It is commendable, we suggest, only when it is necessary to accommodate experience, and only then as a temporary expedient until a better rationality can be developed. Unless, we contend, the well-known incoherence of classical views can be shown to be more consistent with experience in important ways, the superiority in both rational clarity and

coherence of dipolar Process theism should be regarded as an advantage over traditional monopolar views.

(2) Dipolar Process theism is more consistent with at least some ordinary experience. Process philosophy makes it fully possible to affirm the reality of the world. Perhaps some people actually experience the world as a merely derivative or illusory reality, but the ordinary secular experience of most human beings, we contend, rests on the inarticulate, prethematized, assumption that our experience depends upon and at least partially reveals a real world, a world largely independent of our existence and of our experience. And this is a world in which becoming, change, contingency, temporality, and the like are real factors. Further, virtually all of our actions are predicated on the fundamental faith or confidence that what we do makes a real difference, both to ourselves and to others. Such a faith, such basic human experience, makes no sense if the world is either totally determined or totally illusory. And to make a real difference is, we claim, to make a difference to God. But if that is so, God's life must, in some way, be dependent on our acts, thus relative, and all of the other Omega categories.

Earlier in this paper it has been claimed that dipolarity is more consistent with our experience in another way. We observed that the good as we experience it, whether in art or in morals or in knowledge, is always some harmony or balance of Alpha and Omega. Obviously no utterly simple work of art would be interesting, let alone beautiful, but neither would one of pure diversity or chaos. Similarly, human actions based on complete purity of motive and purpose, a purity which consistently fails to take account of diverse motives and interests, is commonly regarded as reprehensible, perhaps even as reprehensible as the characterless behavior of a sociopath. So too with knowledge: we seek an appropriate balance between the simple, clear, and potentially trivial on the one hand, and the complex, rich, and potentially confused on the other. That the experienced good is always to some degree dipolar is not merely the testimony of sophisticated experience but part of the very essence of experienced value; that is, it is a feature of everyone's experience.

(3) The dipolar approach provides a more adequate basis for value theory and for good human action. If cause is in principle

better than effect, if activity is inherently better than passivity, if permanence is to be preferred to change, if one is superior to many, what does this say about human values? What of sensitivity, adaptability, compassion, the spirit of adventure, and community? Are such values to be despised in favor of rigidity, single-mindedness, aloofness, and individualism? It is at least conceivable that the philosophical prejudice in favor of the Alpha categories has encouraged a one-sided sense of values and thereby contributed to the inordinate valuation of power, independence, and ego which is now recognized by so many as a weakness of Western civilization. Some Process philosophers and theologians are now attempting to develop an ethics based on the dipolar view which insists on a proper balance between Alpha and Omega while recognizing the greater inclusiveness of Omega values and virtues. Obviously they have no difficulty utilizing important insights of both environmentalists and feminists.

(4) Dipolar Process theism is more consistent than monopolarity with the testimony of religious traditions. Only through great feats of intellectual manipulation could the father of Abraham, Isaac and Jacob, or Lord Krishna be ultimately identified with pure Being, the Absolute, or Brahman. The very diversity of testimonies within any major, and therefore rich, religious tradition probably precludes the possibility of any philosophical claim to be simply consistent with such traditions. But the God who led his people out of the wilderness of Egypt and entered into covenants with them, who threatened and cajoled them and responded to their wickedness and infirmities; indeed, any God who is love, who cares about the world and its creatures, must be described in a dipolar way, as both Alpha and Omega.

The dipolar view makes evident why any adequate theology needs both philosophy and religion, both reason and revelation. As Alpha, God is necessary, one whose nonexistence could be neither a fact nor even a possibility. But the necessary existence of God and all that flows from it, as Anselm saw, is a matter of conceptual analysis and clarity. Much contemporary philosophy to the contrary not withstanding, God is the central philosophical issue. Precisely because unnecessary existence is never a question of history or fact, the quest for understanding it must lie largely with that discipline which is rightly concerned with fundamental principles and meanings in relation to which factual considerations are neutral—that is, with philosophy. The nature of the divine essence is fundamentally a conceptual problem, requiring conceptual analysis.

On the other hand, God as Omega is largely unapproachable by philosophical analysis. While philosophical analysis might lead to a conclusion that it is possible that God was in Christ, it can never conclude that God was in fact in Christ. Inasmuch as the divine will is to any degree particular, that is, other than absolutely general, it can be known, to whatever degree it can be known at all, only through history, art, and science. Religious traditions are not philosophical systems precisely because it is in their stories and their practices that the concrete richness of divine interaction with the world can be intimated. The dipolar conception of God, in which God is concrete as well as abstract, becoming as well as being, temporal as well as eternal, effect as well as cause, helps us to comprehend intellectually, as monopolar conceptions could not, how this is so, how it is that both the ontological argument and the witness of faith are theologically necessary.

Preeminent perhaps, certainly very prominent, within the witness of faith of many religious traditions is the conviction that God is love. But a God who cannot change or have contingent responses is an individual for whom whatever happens in this contingent world must be a matter of indifference, one who is totally insensitive and unresponsive toward all that happens in this world. Nothing that we do or enjoy or suffer could contribute to the divine life in any significant way, that is, in a way which would make that life any different from what it would have been had our lives been radically different or not at all. This is surely a complete repudiation of divine love in favor of a conception of pure abstract power without love.

Dipolar Process theism stands in some contrast to both classical theism and classical pantheism. But its real virtue lies not so much in that contrast as in its ability to make sense of classical views by incorporating them with a larger, more complex conception of God, a conception which is largely consistent with common human experience and the testimony of faith which directs us toward a more adequate theory of values.

NOTES

1 Alfred North Whitehead, *Science and the Modern World* (New York: Macmillan, 1925), 257.

2 Alfred North Whitehead, *Religion in the Making* (New York: Macmillan, 1926), 90.

3 Alfred North Whitehead, *Process and Reality* (New York: Macmillan, 1929).

4 Charles Hartshorne, *Whitehead's Philosophy* (Lincoln: University of Nebraska Press, 1972), 13-14, 144, 155, 159.

5 For extensive comparisons of Whitehead and Hartshorne see *Two Process Philosophers: Hartshorne's Encounter with Whitehead*, ed. Lewis S. Ford (Chico, Calif.: Scholars Press, 1973); and Gene Reeves, "Whitehead and Hartshorne," *The Journal of Religion* 55, no. 1 (January 1975): 125-37.

6 Hartshorne's use of the term "dipolar" is most fully developed in Charles Hartshorne and William L. Reese, *Philosophers Speak of God* (Chicago: University of Chicago Press, 1953), esp. "Introduction." Though the term "dipolar" is not much used, the dipolar conception of deity is also developed in *The Divine Relativity* (New Haven: Yale University Press, 1948), *Man's Vision of God* (New York: Harper & Bros., 1941), and in *Creative Synthesis and Philosophic Method* (LaSalle, Ill.: Open Court, 1970), esp. chaps. 6 and 11.

7 Paul Tillich, *Systematic Theology* (Chicago: University of Chicago Press, 1951), 1:198-201, 243-50.

8 Morris R. Cohen, *Reason and Nature* (New York: Harcourt, Brace & Co., 1931), 165-68, and *Preface to Logic* (New York: Henry Holt, 1944), 74-75.

God as Process in Whitehead

Bowman L. Clarke

*I*t is generally recognized by Alfred North Whitehead's interpreters that in *Process and Reality*[1] he has two types of process: the genetic process of becoming which is nontemporal,
and the temporal process of transition. Not keeping these two types
of process distinct has, I fear, caused some confusion in interpreting
Whitehead, particularly his conception of God.[2] In this paper I
want to attempt to interpret these two types of process and then to
relate them to Whitehead's conception of God by observing what
the two types of process are in terms of the problem which they are
designed to resolve—that is, the problem of time and change.

Kant in the *Critique of Pure Reason* tells us that time cannot
change, for if time changed there would have to be a time in which
time changed. He writes: "For change does not effect time itself, we
must think yet another time, in which the sequence would be
possible."[3] J. M. E. McTaggart[4] utilizes this fact in order to develop
his paradoxical exposition of time, and as a consequence, concludes
that nothing can be in time. McTaggart presents what A. N. Prior
has called "the phenomenology of time with singular accuracy"[5]
in terms of two series: the A series and the B series. The B series is the
order of events in terms of earlier and later (or before and after).
This ordering of events is, according to McTaggart, "permanent."
This is Kant's time that cannot change. If event *a* is earlier than event

b, then it cannot become the case that it is later than *b.* In contrast, McTaggart's A series introduces change and his subsequent paradox. The A series orders events as past, present, and future. This ordering is not permanent, but according to McTaggart, "transitory." Here there is change: an event is future and then becomes present and then past. Events, despite Kant, do change. McTaggart illustrates this with the event of the death of Queen Anne:

> Take any event—the death of Queen Anne, for example—and consider what changes can take place in its characteristics. That it is a death, that it is the death of Anne Stewart, that it has such causes, that it has such effects—every characteristic of this sort never changes.

This, of course, characterizes the B series, but McTaggart continues:

> But in one respect it does change. It was once a death in the far future. It became every moment an event in the nearer future. At last it was present. Then it became past, and will always remain past, though every moment it becomes further and further past.[6]

And this, of course, if the A series.

Now McTaggart argues that since time involves change, then the B series is essential to change. His argument is as follows:

> Such characteristics as these [an event's being future, becoming present, and becoming past] are the only characteristics which can change. And therefore, if there is any change, it must be looked for in the A series, and in the A series alone. If there is no real A series, there is no real change. The B series, therefore, is not by itself sufficient to constitute time, since time involves change.[7]

It is the A series, which is essential to time, that produces the paradox. This change in the A series, McTaggart argues, produces a contradiction. For an event to be present, it cannot be past and cannot be future. But every event (excluding of course a last event, if there be such) is both present and past; therefore every event is both not-past and past. And McTaggart argues one cannot resolve this problem by producing a meta-time in which this change takes place, as Kant suggested, for the same problem would again arise producing another meta-meta-time, etc. Thus we get in an infinite regress with the same problem recurring at each higher level of time. He then concludes:

> The reality of the A series, then leads to a contradiction and must be rejected. And, since we have seen that change and time require the A series, the reality of change and time must be rejected.[8]

In this paper I would like to propose that Whitehead's two types of process are an attempt to resolve McTaggart's paradoxical character of time and change. There is an intrinsic relationship between McTaggart's A series and Whitehead's genetic process of becoming and between the B series and the temporal process of transition.[9] However, before we consider this, I would like to look at another attempt to deal with McTaggart's paradoxical analysis of time, the development of tense logic. According to Prior, the dean of the subject, tense logic "was provoked in the first place by McTaggart's famous proof that time is unreal."[10] Of course, there are alternative ways of setting up a tense logic, as well as alternative tense logics. But they usually revolve around taking the B series as tenseless, either syntactically or semantically, and characterizing the A series in terms of tensed propositions, so that 'It shall be the case that p' is true at some time, p is true at some later time and 'It has been the case that p' is true at some even later time. At the time when 'It has been the case that p' and the time when 'It shall be the case that p' are true, p itself can be false. And when p is true, 'It has been the case that p' and 'It shall be the case that p' can be false. In short, p can be true at a particular time and false at others. In fact, Prior has characterized tense logic as "an attempt...to give something of the rigor of modern logical systems to a language whose sentences resemble those of natural language in being, in some cases at least, true at one time and false at another."[11] Thus McTaggart's contradiction is avoided by allowing the truth-values of propositions to change with time.

Of course, due to the nature of time, McTaggart was not familiar with these later developments of tense logic. We can only speculate as to what his response might have been. In all likelihood he would have said that tense logic attempts to reduce change to the change in the truth-values of propositions. And then pointed out that this reality does not solve the problem. He was familiar with Bertrand Russell's attempt[12] to resolve the problem by introducing times into propositions so that we have such propositions as, 'My poker is hot at t^1' and 'My poker is hot at t^2'. According to Russell, if the former proposition is true and the latter one false, then change has taken place. But McTaggart points out that if the former proposition including 't^1' is true, it is always true; and if the one containing 't^2' is false, it is always false. Where is the change? McTaggart would, no doubt, point out that the tense logician faces the same problem at a meta-linguistic level. Analogously, if the semantic statement "'My poker shall be hot' is true at t^1" is true, it is always true; and if the semantic statement "'My poker was hot' is true at t^2" is true, it is always true.

It is, however, the charge that to attempt to solve the problem of change by allowing the truth-values of propositions to change is merely to reduce to the change in truth-values of propositions that I want to call attention to, for Prior has an answer to this charge. He writes, for example,

> the changes in truth-value statements and opinions are not properly speaking changes in these statements and opinions themselves, but reflexions of changes in the objects to which they refer (a statement being true when what it says is so, and ceasing to be true when that ceases to be so).[13]

I think this statement is of particular importance because it suggests that tense logic as such solves no metaphysical problems. Of course, it is a known fact that alternative axiomatizations of propositional tense logic reflect alternative conceptualizations of time, which is usually considered a problem of metaphysics. It is with the introduction of quantification, or predicate logic, however, that what Richard Gale[14] has called "hardcore" metaphysics enters the picture with a vengeance. When one introduces quantification over individuals one must face the fact that Queen Anne not only perished, but she came into being and existed during a finite duration. In fact, Prior closes his *Past, Present and Future* with this remark:

> I would like to finish, however, with a philosophical rather than a formal remark, though it may turn out to have a bearing on our

formalisms. The problems of tensed predicate logic all arise from the fact that the things of which we make our predications, the 'values of our bound variables', include things that have not always existed and/or will not always do so.[15]

Thus, the metaphysical problem of becoming and perishing, which Whitehead would take to be McTaggart's problem, cannot be resolved by simply resorting to tense logic.

I have recounted the above as a background for the problems which I take Whitehead to be dealing with in his theory of two processes. Whitehead is frequently characterized as holding an event ontology. This is, I think, an accurate characterization, if what is meant by this is that all other entities can be defined or constructed in terms of events, their properties and relations. In fact, in the closing pages of *The Concept of Nature* Whitehead tells us that "the final conclusion" is "that the concrete facts of nature are events exhibiting a certain structure in their mutual relations and certain characters of their own."[16] If this is true then McTaggart's problem, which is characterized in terms of events and time, is particularly relevant.

An explanation of Whitehead's use of the term 'event' is in order at this point. In his earlier writings up through *Science and the Modern World*,[17] the term is used for "a volume of space through a duration of time."[18] He is not using it in the sense of a space-time point in physics or in the ordinary sense, such as a particular automobile accident. In contrast to the former, events are extended in both space and time; in contrast to the latter, events have definite boundaries in both space and time. Also, events, although extended, are infinitely divisible into smaller events. In *Science and the Modern World*, he begins using the term 'space-time region', or just 'region', as synonymous with 'event'; and in *Process and Reality* he adopts the latter, along with the term, 'quantum of space-time', as the technical term rather than event. The ether of events, all of space-time, in the earlier work is replaced here with the extensive continuum of all regions. The extensive continuum is frequently compared by Whitehead to Plato's Receptical;[19] it is the locus for the instantiation (or ingression) of all forms (or eternal objects). This comparison with Plato is a good one to keep in mind when reading Whitehead.

In *Process and Reality*, the term 'event' is seldom used, but when it is used it is limited to those space-time regions which are articulated as actual entities (actual occasions) and nexūs. Prehensions, for example, are actualized regions and are subregions of an actual entity, but they are not referred to as events. This distinction is due to the fact that teleology has entered the picture and prehensions are incomplete instantiations, or only partial instantiations of the pattern (i.e., subjective aim) of some actual entity. The paradigm of an actual entity is a momentary experience, and the paradigm of a prehension is a feeling in some experience: "subjective experiencing is the primary metaphysical situation which is presented to metaphysics for analysis."[20] A nexūs is a region actualized by a number of actual entities related by physical relations. Despite this distinction between 'event' and 'region', I shall continue in what follows to use the term 'event' for the actualization of any space-time region.[21]

It was suggested earlier that there was an intimate relationship between McTaggart's A series and Whitehead's genetic process of becoming and McTaggart's B series and Whitehead's temporal process of transition. I would like now to make that claim good by suggesting two areas of agreement between McTaggart and Whitehead. The first is that the relationships of events do not change. Whitehead, for example, tells us that "an actual entity never moves, it is where it is and what it is…"[22] This would also apply to prehensions and nexūs. They are where they are and what they are. In the Category of Explanation XX, he tells us that "'Determination' is analyzable into 'definiteness' and 'position,' where 'definiteness' is the illustration of certain eternal objects [i.e., forms, *what it is*], and 'position' is relative status in a nexus of actual entities [i.e., *where* it is in the extensive continuum]."[23] Let us recall McTaggart's discussion of the event, the death of Queen Anne: "That it is a death, that it is the death of Anne Stewart, that it has such causes, that it has such effects—every characteristic of this sort never changes." Since for Whitehead position in space-time is defined according to the Minkowski cones, with reference to causality, Whitehead is in full agreement with McTaggart here. Neither what it is, i.e., a death (the death of Anne Stewart) nor where it is, i.e., having such causes and such effects, can change. The B series is as "permanent" for Whitehead as for McTaggart. Rather than saying, however, that the B series is "permanent," we should say that the 'is' in 'x is before y' is tenseless in the B series. Also, since Whitehead has made room for relativity theory, there are alternative B series or time systems.

Whitehead would also agree that if change is to be found it must be found in the A series. In speaking to Locke's characterization of time as a 'perpetual perishing', he writes: "If he had grasped the notion that the actual entity 'perishes' in the passage of time so that no actual entity changes, he would have arrived at the point of view of the philosophy of organism."[24] Temporal change is due to the becoming and perishing of actual entities (events). The becoming of an actual entity is the ingression of a selection of eternal objects (or forms) in a quantum of space-time (or region) in the extensive continuum. Perishing is the ingression of another selection of eternal objects in a subsequent quantum of space-time, another becoming; and change is the difference between the forms "here-now" and those "there-then." He writes, for example, "The fundamental meaning of the notion of 'change' is the difference between actual occasions comprised in some determinate nexūs."[25] Both the change in position (where something is) and the change in definiteness (what something is) are due to the becoming and perishing of actual entities (events) which themselves do not change. One can easily see why Whitehead identifies his extensive continuum of space-time with Plato's Receptical and quotes with approval Plato's characterization of time as "the moving image of eternity."[26] Time is the changing instantiation of eternal objects. As Whitehead himself puts it,

> In the philosophy of organism it is not 'substance' which is permanent, but 'form'. Forms suffer changing relations, actual entities 'perpetually perish', subjectively, but are immortal objectively. Actuality in perishing acquires objectivity, while it looses subjective immediacy."[27]

It is the last phrase in the above quote, "looses subjective immediacy," that ties the becoming and perishing of actual entities (or events) to McTaggart's A series. "Subjective immediacy" is a "here-now" or a specious present here. What has perished relative to a given "here-now" is its causal past, and what is yet to become relative to a given "here-now" is its causal future. What makes it a "here-now," or specious present here, is its becoming—its genetic process. This characterizing of a "here-now" in terms of its becoming, or its genetic process, goes back to Whitehead's early work, *An Essay Concerning the Principles of Natural Knowledge*. There, for example, he writes,

> natural knowledge is a knowledge from within nature, a knowledge 'here within nature' and 'now within nature,' and is an awareness of the natural relations of one element in nature (namely, the percipient event) to the rest of nature.[28]

All we have to do to translate this quote into the categories of *Process and Reality*, is to replace 'percipient event' with 'actual entity'. What constitutes it as a "*here* within nature" and a "*now* within nature"? Whitehead goes on to explain that these

> relations are perceived in the making and because of the making. For this reason perception is always at the utmost point of creation. We cannot put ourselves back to the Crusades and know their events while they are happening. We essentially perceive our relations with nature because they are in the making.[29]

In short, what characterizes a region in the extensive continuum as a "here-now" is that its relations, which were only possible or potential, are *in the making*, in the process of becoming actual. When the relations of a region, both its relations to other regions and its relations to eternal objects, are potential that region is in the future; when those relations are in the process of becoming actualized (its genetic process), that region is in the present; and when its relations have become actual, it is in the past. Yet none of its relations, neither those which the region has with other regions (its position) nor those which it has to eternal objects (its definiteness) ever change. Change is due to the perishing of one actual entity and the subsequent becoming of another. In this way Whitehead attempts to hold on to change and at the same time avoid McTaggart's subsequent paradox, by agreeing that the characteristics of an event do not change, yet adding that they become actual, constituting it as present, and perish, constituting it as past.

In spite of these basic agreements between Whitehead and

McTaggart, that is, that events do not change their characteristics and that the change which is essential to time must be found in the A series, there is a fundamental difference and it is due to Whitehead's conception of the genetic process. McTaggart, for example, in a footnote in *The Nature of Existence* writes:

> It is very usual to contemplate time by the help of a metaphor of spatial movement. But spatial movement in which direction? The movement of time consists in the fact that later and later times pass into the present, or—which is the same fact expressed in another way—that presentness passes to later and later times. If we take the first way, we are taking the B series as sliding along a fixed A series. If we take the second way, we are taking the A series as sliding along a fixed B series. In the first case time presents itself as a movement from future to past. In the second case it presents itself as a movement from earlier to later.[30]

Whitehead would reject this "spatialization" of time. There are no "fixed" future events, no fixed B series to move into the present. Earlier I suggested that it would be better to say that the 'is' of the relation, x is before y, which orders the B series, is "tenseless" rather than "fixed" or "permanent." To call it "fixed" or "permanent" is to spatialize it and to suggest that it is settled and there in the future ready to become present. Whitehead would insist that there is, to use a term from Richard Gale,[31] an asymmetry between the past and future. The past, relative to a particular event, is fixed and settled; it is what has become actual. The present, relative to a particular event, is what is becoming actual. But future events must wait to see how the present becomes actual. There is freedom, to some degree, in the becoming of any actual entity, and consequently, in any event. Thus the B series becomes fixed in its tenseless manner as events become. There is only "a movement from earlier to later." And this movement from earlier to later along the B series is the second type of process, the temporal process of transition. Whitehead uses this term, 'transition', because if *a* becomes and perishes and *b* becomes, then *a* is before *b*, or there is a transition of the "here-now" from *a* to *b*, and *a* for *b* becomes a "there-then." The process of transition is temporal in the sense that its phases can be ordered by the temporal relation, *x* is before *y*. And this process, characterized by supersession or transition is, according to Whitehead, a "three way process. Each occasion supersedes other occasions, it is superseded by other occasions, and it is internally a process of supersession."[33] Thus the relation, x is before y, can hold between actual entities (occasions), prehensions within an actual entity, or between nexūs of actual entities. The process of transition is the B series taken as a process, what we usually mean by the flow of time.

In contrast, the genetic process of becoming is nontemporal, in the sense that its phases, or stages, are not ordered by the temporal relation, x is before y. In *Process and Reality* Whitehead, for example, insists:

> This genetic passage from phase to phase is not in physical time: the exactly converse point of view expresses the relationship of concrescence [the genetic process of becoming] to physical time. It can be put shortly by saying, that physical time expresses some features of the growth, but not the growth of the features.[33]

We have seen above how physical time, the B series, "expresses some features of the growth": it is the outcome of the becoming and perishing of the actual entities, their prehensions and their nexūs. The phases, or stages, in the becoming of an actual entity, however, are not temporally orderable.

This denial that the becoming of an actual entity (or event) is in physical time is an attempt to avoid Kant's problem: if time changed, then there would have to be another time in which time changed—or to avoid McTaggart's infinite regress of times. The becoming of an actual entity is the becoming, or actualization, of a quantum of space-time. The *becoming* of an event cannot itself be an event. If the *becoming* of an event, *a,* were itself an event, then it would have to be before the event in question, in this case, *a.* But the only events before *a* are events that have become and perished. Therefore, there would have to be some other time in which the event, the *becoming* of *a,* were located. But how about the *becoming* of that event, namely, the *becoming* of the *becoming of a?* We immediately are faced with McTaggart's infinite regress of times. In short, Whitehead denies that the passage from potentiality to actuality in an event is a temporal process.

In *Temporal Logic,* Rescher and Urquhart define a process as "a programmed sequence (temporal sequence) of repeatable state-types."[34] By inserting the phrase, 'temporal sequence', they define a process so that any process belongs to the B series, and would be a process of transition. Later, however, they refer to what they call a "quasi-process": namely, a "coming to be and passing away."[35] This process is for them such a quasi-process. The genetic process for Whitehead is, however, a programmed sequence. It has definite repeatable phases, or stages; they are just not temporally ordered phases. There are essentially three:

(1) The "primary" ("dative," "conformal," "reproductive," "responsive"—Whitehead uses all these terms) phase. This phase is characterized by the ingression of eternal objects which are inherited from past actual entities.
(2) The "supplemental" phase. This phase is characterized by the ingression of novel eternal objects or novel appropriations of inherited ones.
(3) The "satisfaction" phase. This phase is the fully actualized actual entity with all its eternal objects appropriately ingressed.

It is easy to see that these phases are distinguished through the different ways in which eternal objects are becoming instantiated in the given space-time quantum, or region, which is becoming actualized. Whitehead, for example, explains, "The distinction between the various stages of concrescence consists in the diverse modes of ingression of the eternal objects involved."[36] These same three phases are repeated in the becoming of any actual entity, or event. And he wants to use the term process here not only because we have three repeatable phases, but because of the element of decision in any actual entity. It is this element of decision within each actual entity which makes for what we referred to earlier as the asymmetry between the past and future. Given any selection of eternal objects that are inherited from the past, there are always alternative ways in which the event can become actualized or reach satisfaction—and in becoming, it becomes actualized this way, rather than that way. "There are," he writes, "alternatives as to its determination, which are left over for immediate decision."[37]

All of the above is to suggest that in interpreting Whitehead one must carefully distinguish between the passage of an event, which is a process of transition, and the becoming of an event, which is a genetic process. The phases of the passage of an event can all be ordered by the relation, x is before y. The becoming of an event, however, is the informing of the spatio-temporal continuum, and its phases are not so orderable. The becoming of an event is the actualization, or creation, of a quantum of space-time. And as St. Augustine pointed out some time ago, the creation of time, along with the decision that it be this way rather than that, is not itself in time.[38]

For Whitehead, God is an actual entity.[39] This means that God, like any other actual entity, does not change. He is where he is and what he is; he neither changes position nor definiteness. In short, no characteristic or relation of God changes, they merely become. This immediately raises the question: How are the two processes, the genetic process of becoming and the temporal process of transition, illustrative of God? A number of things may be said here in response to this question.

First, as for the process of transition, God is not a spatio-temporal part of a process of transition. There is no actual entity before him and no actual entity after him. He is not located in any B series. For this reason Whitehead refers to God as the "nontemporal actual entity."[40] He is not a member of the field of the relation, x is before y. It is this fact which leads Whitehead to use the term, 'actual entity' in a general sense for both God and finite actual entities, and to use the term, 'actual occasion', for finite actual entities.[41] 'Occasion' has a temporal connotation which 'entity' does not have.

Second, this means that God does not perish as finite actual entities do. His "here-now" is everlasting; it embraces the entire extensive continuum and, consequently, all finite "here-nows." Whitehead came to the realization of this possibility as early as *The Concept of Nature.* In the chapter, "Time," he introduces the possibility of an imaginary being:

> We can imagine a being whose awareness, conceived as his private possession, suffers no transition, although the terminus of his awareness is our transient nature. There is no essential reason why memory should not be raised to the vividness of the present fact... Yet with this hypothesis we can also suppose that the vivid remembrance and the present fact are posited in awareness as in their temporal serial order.[42]

What is suggested here in this imaginary being is the possibility of a percipient event (actual entity) whose present, its "here-now," is co-extensive with the extensive continuum. In comparing our present immediacy to that of this imaginary being, Whitehead goes on to say,

> Thus our own sense-awareness with its extended present has some of the character of the sense-awareness of the imaginary being whose mind was free from passage and who contemplated all nature as an immediate fact. Our own present has its antecedents and its consequents, and for the imaginary being all nature has its antecedents and its consequent durations. Thus the only difference in this respect between us and the imaginary being is that for him all nature shares in the immediacy of our present duration.[43]

The difference between our awareness in the immediate present and the awareness of this imaginary being is in extent. Once one has rejected the concept of an instantaneous present and introduced the notion of an extended present, there is no necessary limit as to its duration. In fact, Whitehead conceives of different types of actual entities as having different durations for a "here-now." Such a specious present could very well embrace all of space and time and not participate in perishing, or what Whitehead here refers to as the passing of nature. It is merely a contingent fact that our "here-now" is limited spatially and temporally, and consequently, is superseded by a new "here-now" so that it becomes a "there-then," or perishes. "Sense-awareness," he writes, "might be free from the character of passage, yet in point of fact our experience of sense-awareness exhibits our minds as partaking in this character."[44]

The only purpose this imaginary being serves in *The Concept of Nature* is to point out that there is no necessary limit to a "here-now." Whitehead is not here concerned with metaphysics; his subject matter in *The Concept of Nature* is philosophy of science. I would suggest, however, that in his later metaphysical works this imaginary being becomes the consequent nature of God—that is, God's awareness of nature. In order to develop into his full conception of God, however, the imaginary being must be supplemented by the primordial nature of God, which in *Science and the Modern World* is introduced as the Principle of Concretion.[45] Here value and teleology enter the picture and we are on the way to a

181

full-blown metaphysics. The primordial nature of God is the envisagement of all eternal objects and "valuations determining the relative relevance of eternal objects for each occasion of actuality."[46] This is God's influence on the finite actual occasions. It takes both God's teleological influence on the finite actual occasions of nature, his primordial nature, and God's awareness of the finite actual occasions of nature, his consequent nature, to complete the full concept of God in *Process and Reality*.

Third, to deny transition of God, in the sense that God cannot be located in any B series, does not deny that there can be transition within God. God, as any actual entity, has supersession within his "here-now." As Whitehead says in the first of the above quotes concerning the imaginary being, "the vivid remembrance and the present fact are posited in awareness as in their temporal serial order." Or, as he says in the second quote, "...for the imaginary being all nature has its antecedent and consequent durations." In short, all the B series are tenselessly in God's consequent nature and there ordered temporally in the vivid immediacy of one "here-now." I have always been suspicious that those who, like Bertrand Russell, R. B. Braithwaite, A. J. Ayer, W. V. O. Quine, or J. J. C. Smart, wish to reduce the A series to the B serie (or series) by declaring the A series to be due only to human subjectivity, are really thinking of omniscience "demythologized."

Fourth, to say that God's "here-now" embraces the entire extensive continuum and cannot be located in any B series, is to say that God "is in unison of becoming with every other creative act."[47] This means that he is in the present of every other actual entity and that every other actual entity is in his present. This fact has serious consequences for any tensed talk about God. How a Whiteheadian tense logic would appear is a fascinating subject. To say the least, it would be highly complex. Since Whitehead's theory of time is designed to accommodate the theory of relativity one would have tenses for the causal past and the causal future, relativized to a "here-now" rather than a mere "now," and it would be extended rather than a mere point-instant. And in addition, one would have alternative tense systems for alternative time systems. In spite of this complexity, however, since God is in unison of becoming with every event, then talk about God in any of the alternative systems would have to be in the present tense. It would not make sense, or it would be false, to say "God has known such and such" or "God shall know such and such." The only true statement would be "God is knowing such and such." It would be a fascinating task to work out a Whiteheadian tense logic in which this would be the case.

If my interpretation of Whitehead's two types of process, along with my four observations of how they apply to his conception of God, is correct, then Whitehead's conception of God in *Process and Reality* is far closer to the classical conception of God than is generally recognized. In fact, his conception of God appears to lie somewhere between, say, St. Thomas's conception and a process view such as that of Charles Hartshorne. In speaking of God's knowledge in the *Summa Theologica*, St. Thomas tells us that

> His knowledge is measured by eternity, as is also His being; and eternity, being simultaneously whole, comprises all time... Hence, all things that are present to God from eternity, not only because He has the essence of things present within Him, as some say, but because His glance is carried from eternity over all things as they are in their presentiality.[48]

And similarly in the *Summa Contra Gentiles,* he explains:

> Something can be present to what is eternal only by being present to the whole of it, since the eternal does not have duration of succession. The divine intellect does not have duration of succession. The divine intellect, therefore, sees in the whole of its eternity, as being present to it, whatever takes place through the whole course of time. And yet what takes place in a certain part of time was not always existent.[49]

And then he goes on to relate God's knowledge to the past and future:

> when it is said God *knows* or *knew this future thing,* a certain intermediate point between the divine knowledge and the thing known is assumed. This is the time when the above words are spoken, in relation to which time that which is known by God is said to be in the future. But this is not future with reference to the divine knowledge, which abiding in the moment of eternity, is related to all things as present to them.[50]

I have quoted St. Thomas here at length, because I think these three quotes tell us much of the similarity and the difference between St. Thomas and Whitehead, as I have interpreted him here. In the first quote, for example, we see a similarity to what Whitehead has called the primordial and consequent natures of God: "...not only because He has the essence of things present within Him, as some say..." [the primordial nature]; "but because His glance is carried from eternity over all things as they are in their presentiality" [the consequent nature]. In fact, if you substitute the phrase, "in one everlasting present," for the phrase, "from eternity," you will have a description of the imaginary being of *The Concept of Nature*. There is, however, a difference between these two natures, or aspects, of God for Whitehead which does not appear to be in St. Thomas— and it revolves around this substitution. St. Thomas sees eternity as being a "simultaneous whole" which "comprises all time" and "does not have duration of succession." And St. Thomas relates eternity to the primordial nature: "This side of his nature is free, complete, primordial, eternal, actually deficient, and unconscious."[51] The term 'eternal' is appropriate here for Whitehead, since the primordial nature "is abstracted from his commerce with 'particulars'."[52] It is only concerned with eternal objects and their instantiation in general, not their particular instantiations. In contrast, Whitehead always uses the term 'everlasting' for the consequent nature. In contrast to the primordial nature, the consequent nature, he tells us, "is determined, incomplete, consequent, 'everlasting', fully actual, and conscious."[53] This difference in terminology between 'eternal' and 'everlasting' is important for Whitehead. It allows God in his fullness to be, in contrast to St. Thomas's simultaneous whole, an everlasting whole, one present, comprising all time and having duration of succession. And since God is one everlasting present which includes every other present, his glance is carried everlastingly over all things as they are in their presentiality. And because of this, I think, Whitehead could agree with the third quote above from St. Thomas concerning God's knowledge and the past and the future. This was what I was suggesting above about a Whiteheadian tensed logic. Such a logic, however, has yet to be worked out. The primary point I wish to make here is that time enters into the ordering of the objects of God's knowledge for Whitehead in a way it does not for St. Thomas. And this is largely due to the way in which Whitehead treats the process of becoming and presentness. Events can be co-present, which are, as a matter of fact, before or after each other. Any present has duration.

In contrast to Whitehead's view of God as one, nontemporal, everlasting present encompassing all time, Hartshorne[54] conceives of God as, in Whiteheadian terms, a personally (temporally) ordered society of actual occasion (or a nexus). In fact, he has been the main inspiration for most of the attempts to revise Whitehead's conception of God along these lines. Hartshorne's characterization of God's perfection in terms of his surpassing all, including his own past states (or occasions) requires this. God's later occasions (or states) surpass even his earlier ones in being more inclusive of value. Here time enters into the very characterization of God and His perfection in a way in which it does not for Whitehead. For Hartshorne God changes in the Whiteheadian sense mentioned above: "The fundamental meaning of 'change' is the 'difference between actual occasions comprised in some determinate event [nexus]'."[55] In our hypothetical Whiteheadian tensed logic, it could be said truly of Hartshorne's God, "God has known such and such," "God is knowing such and such," and "God shall know such and such," in much the same way in which we could say the same thing about ourselves. God is an unlimited sequence of "here-nows" in much the same way as our stream of experience is a limited sequence of "here-nows." In short, what we have in these three conceptions of God might be called, with apologies to Quine, three different levels of temporal involvement by the divinity. St. Thomas has the minimum involvement and Hartshorne the maximum involvement, with Whitehead in between.

NOTES

1 Alfred North Whitehead, *Process and Reality* (New York: Macmillan, 1929).

2 See, for example, Bowman L. Clarke, "God and Time in Whitehead," *The Journal of the American Academy of Religion* 48 (1981): 564-79.

3 Immanuel Kant, *Critique of Pure Reason,* trans. Norman Kemp Smith (London: Macmillan, 1963), 214.

4 John M. E. McTaggart, *The Nature of Existence* (Cambridge: Cambridge University Press, 1927), 2:9-31. The argument here was first presented in an article, "The Unreality of Time," *Mind* 17 (1908): 457-74.

5 A. N. Prior, *Past, Present and Future* (Oxford: Clarendon, 1967), 1.

6 McTaggart, 13.

7 Ibid.

8 Ibid., 22.

9 In saying this I do not mean to suggest that Whitehead was consciously answering McTaggart. Surely, however, he was familiar with McTaggart's position in the 1908 article in *Mind*. Also, Whitehead and McTaggart were friends. In a response to some remarks by friends on his seventieth birthday at the Harvard Club, Boston, Whitehead said: "But it is true I was influenced by Hegel. I was an intimate friend of McTaggart almost from the very first day he came to the University." The "Response" is published in Whitehead, *The Interpretation of Science,* ed. A. H. Johnson (New York: Bobbs-Merrill, 1961), 217.

10 Prior, *Past, Present and Future*, 1.

11 A. N. Prior, *Papers on Time and Tense* (Oxford: Clarendon, 1968), 78.

12 See McTaggart, 14-16.

13 Prior, *Past, Present and Future*, 16.

14 Richard Gale, *Negation and Non-Being* (Oxford: Basil Blackwell, 1976), 16.

15 Prior, *Past, Present and Future*, 174.

16 Alfred North Whitehead, *The Concept of Nature* (Cambridge: Cambridge University Press, 1920), 167.

17 Alfred North Whitehead, *Science and the Modern World* (New York: Macmillan, 1925).

18 Ibid., 103.

19 See Alfred North Whitehead, *Adventures of Ideas* (New York: Macmillan, 1933), 192-93, 240-41, 258.

20 Whitehead, *Process and Reality*, 243.

21 This appears to cause no difficulty here. See, for example, Whitehead, *Process and Reality*, 434-39.

22 Ibid., 113.

23 Ibid., 38.

24 Ibid., 222-23.

25 Ibid., 114.

26 Ibid., 514.

27 Ibid., 44.

28 Alfred North Whitehead, *An Essay Concerning the Principles of Natural Knowledge* (Cambridge: Cambridge University Press, 1919), 167.

29 Ibid., 168.

30 McTaggart, 10-11.

31 See Richard Gale, *The Language of Time* (London: Routledge and Kegan Paul, 1968), 103-85.

32 Alfred North Whitehead, "Time," *Proceedings of the Sixth International Congress of Philosophy* (New York: Longmans Green, 1927), reprinted in Whitehead, *The Interpretation of Science*, 241.

33 Whitehead, *Process and Reality*, 434.

34 Nicholas Rescher and Alasdair Urquhart, *Temporal Logic* (Vienna: Springer-Verlag, 1971), 155. Because most of us use the term 'process' in this sense, that is, a "temporal sense," it is almost impossible to understand Whitehead's use of the term in a "non-temporal" sense.

35 Ibid., 161.

36 Whitehead, *Process and Reality*, 248.

37 Ibid., 435.

38 See St. Augustine, *The Confessions*, trans. Edward B. Pusey (New York: Modern Library, 1949), 252.

39 Virtually all interpreters of Whitehead maintain this is his view, even though a number of them maintain that, in order to remove inconsistencies or to present a more religiously adequate view of God, his view of God in *Process and Reality* must be revised so that God is a personally ordered society of actual entities. See, for example, John Cobb, *A Christian Natural Theology* (Philadelphia: Westminster, 1973); and Delwin Brown, "Freedom and Faithfulness in Whitehead's God," *Process Studies* 2 (1972): 137-48.

40 Whitehead, *Process and Reality*, 11, 47, 73.

41 Ibid., 135.

42 Whitehead, *The Concept of Nature*, 67.

43 Ibid., 68.

44 Ibid., 67-68.

45 Whitehead, *Science and the Modern World*, 250.

46 Whitehead, *Process and Reality*, 522.

47 Ibid., 523.

48 St. Thomas Aquinas, *Summa Theologica*, I, 14, 13. The above quote is from the Aton C. Pegis revision of the English Dominican translation in *Basic Writings of St. Thomas Aquinas* (New York: Random House, 1945).

49 St. Thomas Aquinas, *Summa Contra Gentiles*, I, 66, 7. The above quote is from the Aton C. Pegis translation in *On the Truth of the Catholic Faith* (New York: Doubleday, 1955).

50 Ibid., I, 67, 9.

51 Whitehead, *Process and Reality*, 524.

52 Ibid., 34.

53 Ibid., 524.

54 The Hartshornian theme mentioned here can be found in most of his writings. I would particularly recommend Charles Hartshorne, *The Divine Relativity* (New Haven: Yale University Press, 1948); and *The Logic of Perfection* (LaSalle, Ill.: Open Court, 1962).

55 Whitehead, *Process and Reality*, 114.

CONTRIBUTORS

Milič Čapek Professor Emeritus, Department of Philosophy, Boston University, Boston, Massachusetts

Bowman L. Clarke Professor of Philosophy, University of Georgia, Athens, Georgia

Brian P. Gaybba Senior Lecturer in Systematic Theology, University of South Africa

Jean Higgins Associate Professor of Religion, Smith College, Northampton, Massachusetts

William J. Hill Professor of Systematic Theology, Catholic University of America, Washington, D.C.

Galen A. Johnson Associate Professor of Philosophy, University of Rhode Island, Kingston, Rhode Island

Eugene T. Long Professor of Philosophy, University of South Carolina, Columbia, South Carolina

Nelson C. Pike Chair, Department of Philosophy, University of California, Irvine, California

Gene Reeves Dean and Chief Executive, Meadville/Lombard Theological School, Chicago, Illinois